GW00359558

Attempted Escape
From
Western Civilisation

By
Homebuilt Wooden

Catamaran

Attempted Escape
From
Western Civilisation
By
Homebuilt Wooden
Catamaran

The incredible true story of desperate landlubbers who build a catamaran and escape the stifling grip of civilization

Tim and Kingsley Cox

www.jumbleboat.com

JUMBLE BOAT PRESS

ISBN   978-0-6151-9882-8

Jumble Boat Press
Stony Brook, NY, USA
Jersey, Channel Islands, UK
Copyright © 2008 by Timothy and Kingsley Cox

10 9 8 7 6 5 4 3 2

To Mum and Dad

Thanks for all those trips to St. Catherine

Contents

Appendix

Introduction

This is a book about the building of a wooden sea-going catamaran, and the subsequent adventures of the boat and its builders. It is a fairly accurate account of what actually happened, although the names of the characters and some of the places have been changed to ensure anonymity. It has been written by brothers Tim and Kingsley Cox whose initials appear at the start of their highly individual version of events.

However, this book is more than a travelogue, and much more than an account of how to build a sailing catamaran; it's a book about the struggle to break away from normal expectations. From terrifying early encounters with raging tidal waters of the Channel Islands, to the grim, drug controlled world of an out-of-date mental hospital the brothers doggedly press on with their plan to sail around the planet.

Catastrophic navigational ability, the failure of ancient machinery and perennial poverty all conspire to sabotage the mission. But their almost pathological optimism succeeds, and Jumble, the catamaran, sails, perhaps not around the world, but definitely into hearts.

This wry account is a true story.

In their spare time Tim teaches hang-gliding and paragliding on the South Downs of England (www.flysussex.com), and Kingsley dabbles at computational neuroscience at the State University of New York at Stony Brook, New York (www.syndar.org).

KC and TC

Attempted Escape
From
Western Civilisation
By
Homebuilt Wooden
Catamaran

PART 1

Chapter 1

TC
Lost In Oz

Herbert the crazy East German escapee, and I, Tim Cox, the impoverished English walkabout man, looked out across the still waters of the Queensland lagoon.

"Zer she is!" exclaimed Herbert,

"Zer's our baby!"

He held out both arms in an intense gesture of loving ownership.

There, bobbing gently on a weed encrusted mooring, was a trimaran sailing boat.

She certainly looked neglected.

The plan, according to Herbert, was to borrow this boat for an indeterminate time. To sail up the east coast of Australia, cross the Great Barrier Reef and conquer the Pacific.

It was a completely mad plan. But then I had been travelling alone just long enough to entertain these kind of plans as feasible, even inevitable. I had been attempting a 'walkabout' in the style of the adolescent Australian aboriginal. For three months I had hitch-hiked around Malaysia, Thailand and New Zealand. Nearly everywhere I met strange people. Now I was in Townsville, up the east coast of Australia.

The day before Herbert had ushered me into his secret shed and showed me a beautifully made wooden rudder. I was let in on this fine work of his because I had explained to him that I knew how to sail, and had soon become an indispensable element of his plans. Not that I knew much about this at first.

We looked out across the lagoon in quiet contemplation for a short while, then Herbert whipped off his T shirt with a flourish and waded in, "Come on Tim, I zvill give you a guided tour!"

He sped off in that East German super fast crawl, and I followed in his wake using breaststroke owing to my contact lenses and fear of jellyfish.

We swam round the boat; the central hull and the outriggers plumed great ribbons of weed. The boat was about 10 meters long, all the sails were on board, we could see them through the Perspex windows and the only thing missing was the rudder.

This, however, was no longer a problem. Herbert had measured up and manufactured a perfect replacement in his secret shed.

"So we will need charts, and we will need some sort of weather forecast," I explained to Herbert as we sat back on the sand.

"Ant drink!" added Herbert.

This could be overcome as we were both temporarily employed by a back street Townsville brewery as bottle washers. We used toothbrushes and a solution of, I think, Jeyes fluid. Payment was mostly in the form of beer. Herbert had been a bottle washer for three weeks, and that was two weeks longer than me, and over work we chatted about our lives and future plans. This was how he came to know of my childhood boating adventures and I came to hear of his escapades in the boiler rooms of the East German merchant marine.

The plans for the great trimaran escape took on their own insane momentum. Dry foods and tins were stockpiled. Visits to the library were made to photocopy maps. And it was here that I read about an uncomfortable truth, the season of storms and cyclones was about to commence. To steal and sail away in this boat would not only be illegal; it would be very dangerous.

Herbert was having none of it. He seemed to think I was being unnecessarily pessimistic, even cowardly, or paranoid. At one stage he became so worked up that I got a little worried, and at the same time realised that this was a stupid idea that would see me in some Papua New Guinean gaol, or eaten by sharks. I decided to escape. In the early hours a few days later I was hitching out of Townsville and on my way to Brisbane International Airport, and home.

But the idea of sailing off into the Blue yonder had not died. I resolved to build my own boat and go off and have some legitimate adventures. The Dream was born.

Nascent sailing

With Napoleonic Armies triumphant throughout Europe the British government was anxious to maintain naval dominance. In 1797 an invasion seemed all too possible.

The Channel Islands, only a few miles off the French coast must have seemed like the ideal place to moor a massive, intimidatory, fleet of warships. The absence of suitably large, deep water harbours was seen as no obstacle by the rulers of a growing Empire. They would build them.

Millions of tons of granite would be hewn from the islands and built into giant breakwaters over a mile long. Two of these great pincers would envelop whole bays to house the British Fleet. The trouble was that although they completed two edifices they were on different islands, Alderney and Jersey. So each island was left with only half a harbour. The one on Jersey, at St. Catherine's, was hopelessly exposed to winds from the southwest, whilst the one at Braye, on Alderney, was exposed to the northeast.

Like so many trillion pound defence schemes since, these piers were monstrous white elephants.

It was in the shadow of this imposing red granite monolith that King, my brother and co-author of this book, and I learnt to sail. Even the walk down the slipway was enough to make you hold your breath. At low tide there was a fifty foot drop off the top of the seaward side onto jagged rocks. Aged 7 and 9 we were fairly easily intimidated. Only occasionally did St. Catherine present a friendly face, with fair wind and sunshine, usually at high tide – when most of the rocks in the bay were decently covered up. More often than not a wicked swell was sweeping in from the Atlantic causing the sea level to rise and fall 15ft with every wave. A stiff wind would be howling through the rigging of moored boats and all over the bay vicious rocks would be baring their teeth in haphazard black patches, especially in one far reach of the bay known as Hell's Corner. If a racing course itemised rounding a mark at Hell's Corner the blood would drain from my brother's face and my hands would turn cold and sweaty.

"Do we *have to* go to Hell's Corner?" he would ask, as if the race committee might give us a dispensation to miss out this mark in recognition of our youth and terror.

"I'm afraid so King," I would assert, staring grimly at the course on the Club notice board.

"And it looks like a spinnaker run too!"

This was the final nail in the coffin. A dreaded spinnaker run. A huge unwieldy psychopath of a sail that inevitably led to capsize. I might as well have told him that he was on the Captain's list to be flogged at the gratings to within an inch of his life for spitting on deck. At this he would disappear off for one of his frequent visits to the toilet.

But pride alone would see us dressed up in our regulation 1970's dinghy survival kit. This involved wearing oversized lifejackets with huge collars (we were still squeezing into these self same jackets 10 years later) and oiled wool jerseys which when exposed to water would quadruple in weight in an effort to drag a drowning man down. These jerseys had been knitted by our mother, but by the time this heroic operation was complete we had outgrown them. We felt duty bound to force them on in recognition of the thousands of lovingly made stitches. Around our necks, on nylon bridles, we hung savage stainless steel knives. These were to cut ourselves free from any rigging that threatened to hold us under a capsized boat. We were never quite sure how we would get the wretched things open in this event. But for a while we felt they added to the seamanlike aura. Wellington boots completed the outfit.

King and I sailed a Mirror dinghy, a two man wooden boat with red sails. In rough weather, which seemed to be quite often, Dad and the other fathers would stand up to their ankles in the sea and then, as the next wave rolled in, up to their necks. They would be desperately holding onto Mirror dinghies whilst simultaneously trying to encourage their terrified children to take control and sail off to victory. The art was to wait until the decks of the boat were approximately level with the granite masonry of the slipway and then leap in; at this instant Dad's boot would thunder into the stern of the boat and propel us earnestly into the English Channel. King and I would desperately try to avoid either capsizing (which would have involved being smashed onto the rocks) or luffing and going into the dreaded "irons" (which would have also led, inevitably, to being smashed to bits on the rocks). King's occasional cry of, "I don't think I want to go", would occur just at this critical leap moment. Dad, completely drenched by this stage, would overrule him, "*You have to go!*" and King would courageously jump; although, to his mind, it was plainly an act of suicide.

In fact children who dallied too long before leaping in would often miss and end up clinging to their thwarts perilously close to the wall. Fathers would be yelling all sorts of advice,

"Get in!"

"Kick your legs!"

All to little avail, for their wide-eyed, wailing offspring were beyond earshot.

Remarkably, once clear of the land things usually settled down. The gurgling collywobbles would disappear and we would begin to enjoy ourselves. Once you've ridden out a few big waves and contended with the odd wicked gust you become accustomed to the situation, and are able to look around and take stock.

"Now just where is the first mark of the course?" It was years before I realised quite how shortsighted I was.

This was sailing in 'our own time'. The school in Jersey also had a sailing activity, initially organised by Mr. Nicholson.

School Sailing

Our respect for the sea bordered on paranoia. This was probably due to the fact that neither King nor I were strong swimmers. We attained our scout life-saving badge only by being each other's "victim", carefully disguising the fact that we had difficulty enough keeping our own heads above the water let alone that of some desperate member of the public. Also, at school, the sailing sports option was run by the grim Reg Nicholson. He had deep suspicions regarding The Sea.

Reginald Nicholson had a face that was almost entirely wrinkles. A bit like a St.Bernard dog. He had been a lifeboat man and his constant opinion was that the sea was a wild animal that would eat you given the slightest chance, and this was probably a fair view.

He was reluctantly in charge of sailing at school. Reg had written a book entitled, "The Sea Shall Not Have 'Em". The photocopied manuscript was mandatory reading for all people wishing to sail for their sports activity. It was a grim tome, outlining with stark economy the deaths at sea of numerous Jersey seamen. The main thrust of its survival advice was a) never go to sea unless you absolutely have to, and b) if you absolutely have to then never go sea without a sharp knife hanging round your neck. An important appendix to this advice was that the knife had to be so sharp that your father could shave with it. At one point he was insisting that pupils bring in affidavits from their fathers confirming that they had, in fact, shaved successfully with these knives.

It was at this stage that the Head Master realised old Reg was slipping gracefully into senility. The emphasis on knives was quietly dropped. Carrying them was against school rules; numerous fingers had been cut, fathers injured etc. But this was not before both King and I had equipped ourselves with these lethal devices and had iconised Reg as the Old Man Of The Sea. He died before the myth could be destroyed. The teacher who replaced him, Mr.Le Maitre was an immature simpleton in comparison. A gutless, knowledgeless parasite who had never saved a life at sea, let alone in a Force 10 gale on a lee shore. We held him in low esteem.

We actually learnt almost nothing at school about sailing. We were taught instead by Jersey's ex Head of Police, Mr.Le Brocq, almost as old as Reg Nicholson. He too died before he could witness his protégés' sailing triumphs.

By this stage Mum and Dad had decided that their sons' efforts merited a boat and we purchased a Mirror dinghy called "Jocar". There was a thriving fleet of these boats at the local Club and every Sunday we turned up to race. And we would race, we soon realised, regardless of the weather. Honour was at stake, and sailing soon cut us apart, in our eyes anyway, from mere mortals. Other children might have a non-descript weekend watching some sad B movie, whilst we had defied the elements, battled a fragile wooden boat through a tempestuous sea and finished within the final 30 of a hardened racing fleet. Now that was living. It was the beginning of an obsession which lives with us forty or so years later.

KC
More Nascent sailing

The trip from our house to the sailing club wasn't very far, perhaps 15 minutes, but there was plenty of time to develop a keen anxiety about the state of the sea. At seven years old even one 'white horse' is one too many and as we approached the curve in the coast road that gave the first sneak preview into St. Catherine's bay, I was white knuckled in the rear of the car alongside Tim, fervently wishing that the sea would be flat, preferably like a mirror, and the wind slight. On the rare occasions that this was the case my worries would be gloriously swept away to be replaced with an inner calm. When, however, on that first nervous glimpse of the bay, conditions were not to my liking I would enter a denial mode which would be tested several times as the sea revealed itself in greater and greater fullness on approaching the club. Finally we would arrive and my make believe world of ripples and zephyrs would be brutally demolished by the reality of wind, spray and white horses. Dad wasn't going to send us out in *that* was he? Our father had decided that, in order for us to develop moral fibre and avoid becoming saps, we needed to do something that would test us. That something was sailing. I'm not sure how our parents picked this sport since they themselves had never even been in a sailing boat. Perhaps it was the availability of a knackered old Mirror dinghy, but it was certainly dangerous enough for me.

We were taught to sail by Mr. Le Brocq, an archetypal old sea dog who had a heavily lined and lived in face. He had an old lugger moored in the bay and he sedately rowed my brother and me, out to it on a string of Saturday mornings. When we got to the boat, we would painstakingly go around it carefully unclipping the cover and then neatly fold it. Eventually we would get in the lugger, hoist the sails, and sail around the bay a few times with Mr. Le Brocq telling us what the ropes were for and what this and that were called. I never got to grips with all the terms and the only one I remember, apart from the 'sheet', is the 'painter', a piece of rope that attaches a dinghy to the shore. I had been very impressed by the alternative use of the word. We went out in most weather, including conditions that I would have considered foolhardy (i.e. most conditions), but Mr. Le Brocq was in charge and he exuded confidence and complete mastery of anything nautical. To be perfectly honest, I don't think I really took in much during those Saturday mornings, mainly because we were a bit in awe of Mr. Le Brocq, not only because he had the presence of Poseiden himself, but also due to the fact that we had been told he had done some very brave deeds during the second world war.

Our inattention resulted in us being woefully prepared for our maiden trip alone. We rigged our vessel, a 12 foot Mirror dinghy which has a mainsail and a jib, on a Sunday afternoon and wheeled the boat down the very long St. Catherine's slipway to the sea. We were dressed in normal clothes and plimsoles plus a lifejacket, but perhaps wetsuits, wetsuit boots, and spray smocks would have been more appropriate. Just getting the boat off the slipway was no easy matter since waves would pile up along the immense breakwater and break at the launch point. Tim and I got wet to our armpits immediately. Dad held the boat as we clambered in and then pushed us off and away. Sundays were race days so there were other boats milling around together with, fortunately for us, a guard boat. We weren't out very long, floundering around getting in the way of everybody, when I noticed that we were not going forwards anymore. The sails were full and the Mirror was moving through the water, but we seemed to be going backwards. We had ventured out too far and were now in the grip of a strong tide which swept past the breakwater. Also, since we didn't really know how to prepare the boat, the bungs had not been put into their respective holes and the water that came aboard began to fill up the buoyancy tanks. We were clearly sinking. Being frozen to the marrow was the least of our problems – the whirlpools of death at the end of the breakwater were about to swallow us. I was totally terrified. Then, just at it seemed that all hope was lost and we had been forsaken by everyone, the guard boat appeared and dragged us to safety. This, then, was our initiation into sailing and I don't think I had been more scared in my life. Tim had been bricking it too. When we arrived back at the slipway Dad was, despite the fact that we had required to be rescued, pleased to see us. He had been under strict instructions from Mum to bring us back alive. Of course, at this point I should have elected to pursue a safer sport but that was out of the question since my brother professed to Dad that it had all been rollicking good fun. Naturally I couldn't lose face and cheerfully enquired as to when we could go out again. I could feel that moral fibre developing already. In the next few weeks we improved to the point that we rarely forgot the bungs and even began to race, if you could call it that, against other Mirror sailors at the club.

Mirror dinghies could be tuned by the clever adjustment of various pieces of rope. Sometimes, completely serendipitously, we got it right and were temporarily competitive. One of those times clearly stands out as the zenith in the annals of Cox Brothers racing. It was a Sunday, as usual, and there were two races, one class race and a 'pursuit race'. Our main rivals in a Mirror were the Sutcliffe brothers, similar in age to us, and they had without doubt the most spectacular Mirror dinghy in Jersey, possibly even the whole U.K. It had been lovingly built by a master boat builder to be the last word in competitive Mirrors. Each piece of wood, every thwart and spar had been shaped and planed to be right on the border of class rules. The boat was so light that it had to have some lead weights placed down by the centreboard casing in order to be legal for racing. We always suspected that the boat was still illegal since the weight was now unfairly distributed. There probably should have been even more lead. The finish was immaculate with not so much as a single stray brush hair embedded in the varnish on the bottom. Mr. Sutcliffe, a brash Yorkshire man, wanted his sons to win and so brand new sails were provided. Unfortunately for us, the Sutcliffes were also good sailors and so they, in fact, usually won. After a race, when all the boats would come back to the slipway, Mr. Sutcliffe made sure nobody was in any doubt of the outcome.

"Did you win then, sons?"

"Yes, Dad, we think so."

"You mean, you were ahead of all the rest? Well dun lads. Well dun."

All of this was delivered in a loud Yorkshire accent. We really wanted to beat the Sutcliffes, if only to shove it down Mr. Sutcliffe's throat, but it was a very difficult proposition. There were two main problems; one was that their boat, 'Bloomers', could point higher than us which meant they had a great advantage when sailing close to the wind (of course if we had properly tuned our boat, 'Jocar', by raking the mast back then we would have pointed higher too), and secondly, they were better at spinnaker handling than us. Often we would be in the lead half way round only to see Bloomers inexorably getting closer and closer until finally they would overtake us. We had beaten them once, but this was only because they had been rammed and nearly sunk by an Enterprise dinghy which rendered the victory a little hollow.

On this Sunday, however, for reasons that I still don't fully understand, things were different. The build-up routine was the same as ever; nervously rigging the boat trying to quell the collywobbles and then that long walk down the slipway to the launching point. All the usual suspects were there including of course the Sutcliffes, who were putting the final polish on the bottom of Bloomers; Maurice and Natalie Stone, a clueless brother/sister combination who had the rare distinction of, at the start of one light wind race, never crossing the start line and actually moving backwards away from it; the Cripps, a middle aged couple who had, sadly, never made it out of a child's boat; Stuart Breeze; and us. In total there were about 10 Mirrors.

The first unusual event, which was a harbinger of good things to come, was that we made it out to the start line before the race actually began. Our start was very good, also unusual. We were, to use Mr. Sutcliffe's phrase, 'ahead of all the others' (especially the Sutcliffes) at the first mark, and increased our lead up to the second mark. Then the Sutcliffes began to close the gap. On the run my standard feebleness with the spinnaker allowed them to catch right up and, in a wink, they were past us and storming down to the penultimate mark, all cocky. Then it happened. We began to catch up. This was very odd since once they were ahead we generally never saw them again. But this time we were catching them, there was no doubt about it. They were looking puzzled and when we got to within a boat's length puzzlement turned to worry. The older brother began to bark orders to the younger one to pull the jib in, push it out, lean out more, stay in the boat. Nothing helped and we slid by them on the leeward side. This was all the more amazing because the windward boat usually blankets the leeward one, cutting off the wind. It was as though we had our own private breeze. All hell broke loose on Bloomers with the older Sutcliffe yelling at his brother, telling him to put the spinnaker up. That was crazy since we were both sailing too close to the wind for it to fill properly. Of course it drooped and was no help. This was naturally all the younger brother's fault and the shouting continued. Tim and I just held our breath. Once we were far enough ahead we tacked and made the last mark, North buoy, ahead of them and we held our lead until the finish. After crossing the line we glanced behind. There was quite a commotion occurring on Bloomers with the older brother, apoplectic with rage, bashing the younger one over the head with what looked like an oar. Victory was sweet indeed.

There was no sign of Mr. Sutcliffe on the slipway. In the afternoon we won the pursuit race too, where all types of boat race each other on a handicap basis with the slowest boats starting first. We even beat Mr Le Breton, who was the best sailor in the club, possibly the world, by about 5 feet.

We never reached those extraordinary heights again and over time it became obvious that we probably wouldn't be Olympic material.

Eventually I came to terms with sailing and began to enjoy it, even the dangerous edge. We got quite good at racing but were handicapped by two things; nobody had taught us how to tune the boat which of course would have made a huge difference, and I was almost incapable of controlling the spinnaker, much to Tim's disgust.

After spending six years in a Mirror dinghy we graduated to a Fireball. It was like going from a Trabant to a Ferrari. Whereas a Mirror is a solid slow little starter boat, the Fireball is like a cheetah. We really had no business to be in one and we spent a lot of the time careering out of control and endlessly capsizing. Racing the Fireball was also subject to the above 2 handicaps. We named it 'Spirit of Zimbabwe' as a sort of joke but it didn't go down well with the other members of the club and they practically excommunicated us. They thought we were left wing hippies.

Chapter 2
KC
Money..

Paying for the Fireball involved doing summer jobs such as being a plongeur in a nearby restaurant, an assistant nurse in the local mental hospital, and doing virtual slave labour for Ace Cleaning Limited.

As regards experiencing the life of a kitchen skivvy, we had to look no further than La Gaviota, the restaurant next door. From our house we had an excellent view of the back of the kitchen, where all the nasty business of catering occurred. We had delightful vistas of large industrial bins overflowing with stinking decaying vegetable and animal matter, as well as being able to scrutinize the questionable habits of La Gaviota's employees. The back door of the kitchen would swing open frequently to allow the chefs, sous-chefs and even lower staff to smoke, dump waste, stand around picking their noses, or simply do nothing. Whilst the door remained open for a few minutes one could see inside the kitchen itself; dirty white tiles on the floor and walls and many stainless steel sinks with water always running and slopping everywhere. Altogether, it was very reminiscent of a public lavatory.

On the other side of the restaurant, where the customers entered, it was of course a very different scene. Bouquets of roses, clean floors, calming music, and cream teas in fine china. Joe, the proprietor, agreed to take Tim and me on as kitchen helpers for an unbelievably low hourly wage. We were introduced to Miguel, the chief plongeur, who was unable to tell us our duties since he couldn't speak English. Instead, he spoke in Portuguese and complemented this by pointing at the mop and bucket, and the commercial dishwasher. Although he looked like a village idiot, we soon discovered that Miguel had a special talent. He had a deep aversion to any sort of work and it was initially puzzling how he hadn't been fired a long time ago. His talent, it turned out, was similar to that of a dog who seems to know when its epileptic master is about to have a fit; Miguel knew by some mysterious means when The Boss, Joe, was about to appear. He would suddenly, from complete inactivity, become the model of an industrious worker, pushing us aside in his haste to load the dishwasher. Sure enough a few seconds later Joe would appear in the doorway catching Tim and me standing around stupidly gawping at the possessed Miguel. In time we were able to use Miguel like a miner's canary – I would always have a mop handy so I could be ready if I saw him so much as flinch out of the corner of my eye.

The kitchen was truly disgusting. There was grease everywhere, especially on the floors, making them super slippery and dangerous. Somehow, Tim got himself promoted to the heady heights of waiter leaving me stuck with the despicable Miguel and mountains of dirty saucepans to wash up.

Ace Cleaning was slightly better paid but just as crushingly tedious. I was working under the tutelage of an Irishman and we were a team; I did the work whilst he 'supervised', occasionally demonstrating an advanced cleaning technique. One of our jobs was to clean a whole primary school, which was a stupendous amount of work. Still, it would have been all right except that he became fixated on the grout between the floor tiles, which of course was black with dirt. I spent hours on my knees scraping out the dirt with one of those triangular paint scrapers. It would have been faster to regrout the tiles. When he came back from 'supervising' a pint of lager, I had hardly moved, and the scraper was close to circular.

Tim's efforts at making money took a different line….

TC

St. Saviours Hospital

Jersey possessed a vast mental hospital. The imposing granite façade had been constructed by the Victorians to impress and subdue. Inside, the high ceilings and long corridors created a grim, prison-like atmosphere. The building was set back from the road and approached by a long curving drive, and the site surrounded by spiked, black, wrought iron railings.

For some reason, mostly to do with trying to finance sailing boats, I applied to become an auxiliary nurse at this establishment. The job was tolerably well paid and had a socially constructive aspect that appealed to my naively idealistic side. The Administrator who interviewed me kept asking me if I was absolutely sure if I knew what I was letting myself in for.

"Oh yes", I said.

I was assigned to Primrose Ward, a locked ward for insane men. My uniform was one of those white aprons that buttons up down one side, and we were not allowed out the front in case we frightened the public. The entire staff on the ward were Scottish and all smoked with a passion.

On day one I was ushered in by Malcolm, the staff nurse on duty, and the door locked behind us. Almost immediately a huge man with greased black hair lunged towards me and held me by both shoulders,

"Are you my father?" he implored, his frighteningly intense blue eyes piercing into mine.

"No," I assured him, shaking my head.

"Father!!" he insisted.

Malcolm interceded at this point,

"That's enough Brian, go back into the lounge."

Brian retreated backward eyeing me with amazed incredulity. I looked at him similarly.

As the youngest member of the team on Primrose Ward I was delegated the role of toilet and bath attendant. Of a twelve hour shift I would spend at least eight in the toilets. Our inmates consisted in the main of pensioners who were senile or suffering the effects of alcoholism; others had brain damage or some psychiatric problem. There were about thirty of them and none of them could be trusted in the toilets alone.

I hadn't quite realised that my role as auxiliary nurse would devolve to toilet attendant. It was all a bit of a shock. I would place little old men onto toilets, as many as four at a time, and then wait for success. This could take some time.

Occasionally the taut, drum like belly of some poor little old man would betray severe constipation. In this instance Malcolm, the staff nurse, would administer powerful enemas. The recipient would sit on the toilet for what seemed hours. And I would be left on guard. One man, in particular, would stare unflinchingly ahead as the first eruptions began to take hold, initial farts would give way to more extended blats and blubbers of expulsion. The process could continue for a seemingly impossibly long time, massive guffs and explosions would take place all without any expression from the patient. He could have been at the Opera. At first it was all a little unnerving but its amazing how quickly one becomes inured.

One insidious aspect of the job was the smell. Tobacco smoke and Jeyes disinfectant has a powerful aroma that permeates into the very skin. Even after showering the ponk lingered. There was no escape.

One poor gentleman had been an architect, but during an open heart operation had suffered brain damage. Now he could barely walk and clung to his Zimmer frame in terror. His poor wife would come to visit him and tears would stream down both their faces when it was time for her to leave.

In truth it was a tough job, not made any better by the fact that the hospital was a little behind the times. A padded cell still existed on the ward, although I didn't see it used. Control of patients was exercised through drugs, chocolate and cigarettes. Bad behaviour was punished by tobacco suspensions, and if you didn't smoke when you came in you soon did. The high ceilings were stained yellow with nicotine, even the bars on the windows felt sticky with the stuff.

After about two months the strain of getting up at 5.30 am every morning to moped across the island in the pitch dark was beginning to get to me. The antics of my ancient Garelli moped made things worse, the engine took near super-human efforts of endurance to start, only later experiences with outboard motors came close to replicating the dogged belligerence of this machine. The chain would leap off at any opportunity; frequently I would arrive with oily hands and bathed in sweat. The whole set up appeared archaic, it seemed wrong to mix the senile, with the brain damaged, with the mentally ill. I made my observations to the Ward head. Her advice was to keep my head down and don't drink the tea.

One day I was summoned to the main office and told that, after due consideration, it was decided that I probably didn't have the makings of a full time auxiliary psychiatric nurse. It was an immense relief.

I walked outside and gulped in the air a free man. I had learnt a lot. Especially how grateful one should be for sanity, and how easy it is to lose it. Alcohol seemed a fairly easy way to end up mentally incapable.

On my last day at work I asked to be shown the locked ward that adjoined ours. Inside, out of the public view, lived all kinds of deformed and contorted human beings; I had no idea that this kind of place existed. It all confirmed my feeling that there is no innate justice in the world; some people are just horrifically unlucky. In the years since I worked in St. Saviour's I hope, and trust, that things have moved on.

KC

The monies gleaned from all these hardships were put toward the Fireball fund. Tim's heroic and sanity-testing efforts at the mental hospital meant that we were finally in a position to purchase one weary old Fireball. It came with a road trailer, a suite of very old and worn sails, and the heaviest launching trolley in Christendom.

We spent a whole winter stripping and lovingly repainting the Fireball. This necessitated commandeering the garage. Our parents were happy to tolerate this restriction to movements in their own house. Sailing was good and to be encouraged since, up to this point at least, it had kept us out of borstal. Of course, in retrospect, all that work getting the boat's hull as smooth as a baby's bottom, admirable though it was, would have been better spent discovering how to set up the 'rig'. There was a whole area of boat tuning that we knew nothing about and it involved adjusting the mast, stay tensions, and 'spreaders' so that the sails would be the correct shape. If you didn't do this then the boat would be slow compared to a properly tuned Fireball; it would be as if they had four gears when you only had three. Our main competitor at the club, Jeff White, understood the mysteries of Fireball tuning and always beat us. We blamed this lack of success on leaking buoyancy tanks and an older boat (naturally nothing to do with innate skill). Another critical component on the Fireball that nobody had told us about was the 'kicking strap'. This pulley system connects the base of the mast to the boom. It can be tightened to reduce twist in the sail. It needs constant adjustment depending on the point of sailing and wind strength. We thought we were doing well just to have it connected.

Travel, and attempts at higher education interrupted the progress of our sailing. I decided to better myself by studying, of all things, chemistry at university. Far from the anticipated relaxing three year holiday of beer and endless late night philosophical musings with my fellow students, a chemistry degree turned out to be like a 9-5 job with constant lectures and exams. Instead, it was Tim who had the holiday because he sensibly chose English and thus had plenty of time to quaff voluminous amounts of alcohol etc.

Chapter 3

TC
Genesis of Jumble 1985

On my return to England from the Southern Hemisphere, cold sleet showers convinced me of the urgency to escape once more, this time by boat. Being without any money whatsoever I secured a job with a government enterprise to lever the hardcore habitually unemployed from lethargy. It was called the Community Programme, and to qualify all you had to do was live, and be unemployed.

My job involved taking fairly unwilling pensioners from old peoples' homes and introducing them into local community initiatives such as the YMCA Thursday Afternoon Club.

Bizarrely this activity devolved into a fairly serious gambling syndicate. My only three recruits were all vintage diabetics, each singled out by the fact that their disease had resulted in their legs being amputated. The other unifying feature was their passion for cribbage and gambling. Sid, Des, and Larry would sit round the YMCA card table in wheelchairs (I was the only one with legs, let alone a chair) and cheat like hell. The job allowed reasonable latitude to pursue other activities – such as building a boat.

Each week I scoured the yachting press for vessels capable of an extended ocean cruise but simultaneously within my budget of 800 pounds. I even viewed a few vessels. In Brighton Marina I was shown over a small Westerly, this did not take long since it was only 23ft. in length. The owner, clearly desperate to sell, assured me that this type of boat would circumnavigate with ease. Neither of us could stand upright in the cabin so the conversation took place at an awkward angle.
"Oh yes," he enthused, "take you anywhere this boat; she'll shrug off seas like a dog shaking off the rain after a…walk in the park".
Drips of rain pattered down my neck from the closed hatch cover. I decided to keep looking.

Finally a friend of mine, Paul Willis, suggested that I would have to build my own from plans. Desperately poor people inevitably build ocean going vessels from plans. Plans can cost only a few pounds, but they are only one step on from daydreams. Plans come easy, for instance, plans for a base on Mars.

Then fate interceded, in the very next issue of Practical Boatowner there was an advert for plans, (accompanied by wood glue and 4000 bronze nails) for the partially complete hulls of a Wharram Tanenui 28. The perfect boat!

I borrowed my parents' VW Beetle in a delirium of excitement. Within an hour of leaving the ferry I was coasting to a halt on the hard shoulder of the M25. The Beetle had died. I opened the rear engine compartment and wiggled a few leads in desperation.

Having exhausted my thin repertoire of engineering solutions I sheltered out of the rain in the driving seat. After a few moments a van drew up behind me. I began rehearsing my excuses to the policeman. Why it was exactly that I was driving a vehicle registered in Jersey, and did not belong to me. However the van contained not the police, but an AA repair man. Remarkably he accepted my story about having AA family membership and like a wizard replaced the faulty part. I thanked him with the passion of a man saved from hell by the intercession of some passing saint.

The Wharram sat upside down in the garden of a house just outside Colchester. Its builder was moving to New Zealand and no longer had need of two half built catamaran hulls. He promised to deliver the hulls on a flatbed lorry, and I promised to give him all my money.

After shaking on the deal and parting with a cash deposit, I drove on to visit the grandparents. They lived in the remote Suffolk village of Stanton, near Bury St. Edmunds. I was greeted like a long lost grandson, and my plans for constructing a sailing boat received lavish support. Things, so far, were looking good. I fell to sleep under the ancient oak beams of their haunted Tudor cottage, my head full of plans.

Only the small problem of where, exactly, I was going to complete this boat remained. This is how my acquaintance with the Bembridge family took a deeper turn.

The Bembridges

The Bembridges were an extraordinary family. Harold Bembridge was a GP, good looking and relentlessly enthusiastic. He played squash and did most of the cooking. I think his domesticity was some sort of perpetual penance thrust upon him for a) having had an affair and b) impregnating Patricia, his wife, with twins when she truly didn't want any more children.

Their second son, Alan, shared a house with me when we were students and it was he who suggested that I could construct the catamaran in his parents' extensive suburban back garden. Alan was a lean figure of a lad, with the ghostly good looks of an anaemic smoker. He was very committed to smoking. His first and last inhalations of the conscious day took the form of smoke. I say 'day' loosely because, in the winter especially, he rarely saw daylight. Watching movies all day and late into the night he often wouldn't emerge from bed till after sundown.

Patricia, his mother, was similarly keen on smoking. During the week she worked as a midwife and in the gaps she smoked.

Harold seemed a bit bemused by the variations in his six children. They ranged from almost pathologically slothful to wildly energetic.

In retrospect the indulgence of the Bembridges in my boat building efforts was beyond the call of human duty to the poor. Most weekends I arrived like a maelstrom in their house, devastated their garden, ate their food, raided their alcohol supplies, led their youngest daughter astray, and overstayed my welcome.

Patricia Bembridge pursed her lips slightly incredulously as I explained that she would barely notice the boat at the bottom of her garden. The work, I assured her, would be complete within a maximum of three months, maybe sooner with good weather. Harold was wonderfully laid back and positive. If they had but partly realized the disruption the project was going to cause. I had to be tough, with a mission like this heroic sacrifices had to be made. It rains a fair deal in Tunbridge Wells and boat building requires the dry. Within weeks I had constructed a fourth-world polythene shanty town. Roofing battens formed the frame of a lean-to stretching 30ft by 30ft nailed to the massive holme oaks and guyed by lengths of bailing twine. Where the polythene sagged great pools of green mildewed water gathered, and tarpaulins were mustered as leak repairs.

Patricia's enthusiasm was the first to wane, especially when the project shot past an optimistic three month deadline and into the second year. This obviously had something to do with the transformation of her beautiful garden into an earthquake refugee centre.

Very soon the whole edifice seemed to cover about a quarter of an acre, and closely resembled a war zone, or long abandoned scrap yard, half-completed hulls were supported on piles of old tyres. The grim spectacle brought tears to Patricia's eyes when she ventured down beyond her smoking lounge. She had to do this occasionally as I needed to rope in every able bodied hand when I had to turn over a hull.

At first this was considered a bit of an adventure, rolling over a 28ft. catamaran hull. Wellington boots and gloves were donned by the entire household and the job was soon done. But as the weeks rolled into months people had a habit of disappearing when I suggested the task needed doing again. Patricia would just stare at her breakfast bowl and the cigarette would gently vibrate in her hand. It spoke a thousand words.

I had a crack at turning the hulls on my own. I piled tyres up on one side and levered a hull up to the point of no return. As I nipped round to adjust the tyres the hull began to fall, I desperately tried to push it back but it forced me down like a bug beneath a swat. The whole thing bounced on the tyres, fortunately leaving just enough room for my chest cavity. I slowly wormed my way out thinking, "I need help", emotionally, financially and mechanically.

The eldest Bembridge child was David, an erudite bookworm who also enjoyed cycling a tandem at lunatic speeds. He introduced me to books by Olaf Stapleton, a 1930's philosopher who played out his theories in early science fiction dramas. In one book a telepathic child genius sails around the world in a remarkable craft of his own design, collecting similarly odd ball people from around the world. They form an alternative society.

I imagined that this boat could do just such a thing, only without the genius.

The Bembridges II

John, the youngest Bembridge, was strangely impassioned about his CD system. In 1986 this was cutting edge technology and his immaculate speakers did indeed produce a sound quality unsurpassed at the time. He was uncharacteristically protective of this system, white anti-static gloves would be required to handle the discs, the speakers would be dusted, and the unit occupied a sacred space, like a Buddhist shrine, within John's utterly chaotic room.

Sometimes I would be invited in to listen to" ZZ Top" at considerable volume; we would sit cross-legged on the floor in due reverence. I hadn't been so re-enthused about music since King brought back a tape of Pink Floyds' "Dark Side Of The Moon" back in 1973, when he was 10 and I was 12. His friend Tom Devlin had a precocious musical taste and had introduced him to this recording. Apparently it needed to be listened to in pitch darkness while lying flat on your back. I knew this was really another world of music, rich, and wonderful. It was so completely different to anything I'd heard before; as though we'd been allowed a glimpse of a fabulous city where everything was alien to our senses but intoxicating nevertheless.

John and I never quite re-enacted that moment but his music collection certainly eclipsed mine.

When the Bembridges departed on a camping holiday in the summer of '86 they left me, with typical trust and generosity, the run of their house. An unspoken condition was that, under no circumstances, was John's stereo system to be compromised.

The temptation to listen to John's CD collection was obviously too great to endure. And, naturally, it soon occurred to be that it would be pleasant to listen to the Beatles or the Eurthymics whilst working on the boat. I dared not move the machine nearer the boat as it would inevitably get smeared with two part resorcinol resin, and so I initially settled on turning it up full volume and leaving the windows of John's second storey room wide open. But the result was still partially muted. The solution, I found, was to place the speakers on the broad Victorian windowsill and allow half of Tunbridge Wells to appreciate good music. This state of affairs could not, of course, continue.

It was a warm August morning, Annie Lennox of the Eurythmics was just getting into a full-blooded wail in the bit where her heart is being messed with, and I was in mid saw stroke on the rear deck, when silence suddenly prevailed. It was one of those moments when time grinds on only slowly, albeit inevitably. I looked up at the house to see one falling speaker pull the second speaker from their ledge by the wire and crump, out of sight, into the garden. My first thought was that this could not possibly have happened. Nobody would enter the house and push them off. Why not just pull out the plug? Eventually I realised that the speakers had vibrated themselves to their doom, a kind of suicide.

A desperate repair to the system was attempted, the fall had been partially broken by a camellia bush, but the plastic padding looked bulbous, and the matt black paint not quite in keeping, and the bass had a kind of hollowness to it. I don't think John ever forgave me.

Things could have been worse. Jane Bembridge's (the Bembridges' eldest daughter) French exchange student could have actually died when she passed out whilst painting the forward anchor locker. Emmanuelle was a girl of slight build, and whilst I could only access the locker by leaning headfirst down the hatch, she could get in entirely. She volunteered to go in with a brush and bilge paint, and set to work, cheerfully at first and then in complete silence. I had to haul her out, senseless, by her armpits. Never paint in an unventilated space. Later we read about the tragic deaths of an entire family who had slept aboard their half completed boat and been asphyxiated by the carbon monoxide given off by a faulty heater.

Even though I evidently tested their patience and exploited their resources, the Bembridges remained marvelously polite and tolerant. My initial estimate of three months proved ridiculously optimistic.

Everything takes so much longer than the plans suggest. I remember looking at my sketched out timetable; it had statements like,
"screw on bulwarks trim – one day."

This took over three weeks! The hard wood trim first had to be cut and sanded into the appropriate shape and then bent to the curve of the bulwarks whilst being glued, nailed and screwed home. The task required almost super human strength and patience, and huge numbers of vices and clamps. It took a long time because there was about 120ft of trim, each side of the boat being over 28ft. long. Every job on a catamaran is always doubled! And this was a relatively minor job.

Timetables, flippantly formed on a side of A4 in an evening, were hopelessly flawed. Item 4, Day 8: construct 4 hatch covers. In your dreams! Just building the frames for a hatch cover took three days! Actually getting a hatch cover to fit in place took at least four hours per hatch. Obviously, a fundamental and deep-seated deficit of carpentry skills contributed to this missing of project targets.

Chapter 4

TC
Carpentry

After a weekend's frantic labour on the boat I would have hands like those of a bare fist fighter. Graunched and bloodstained, with swollen thumbs, and everywhere the residue of two- part resorcinol glue. This brown glue came in two great five gallon drums; you mixed it together in any handy plastic receptacle and then just waited to get it all over yourself. The glue somehow made its presence felt on virtually every garment I possessed, from underpants to socks.

The problem lay in the fact that, once two equal parts were mixed, the glue would set rock hard within minutes. Haste in its application led to the inevitable accidents and 'comprehensive adhesion', namely glue on everything from shoes to eyebrows.

There was, however, one glorious advantage to this kind of construction, the glue's ability to fill quite large gaps. With the judicious addition of woodchips, hideous miscalculations in measurement and sawing could be covered up. Indeed once the top decks had been covered in nylon fabric (recycled net curtains glued on with resorcinol glue- what else?) who was to know they had been hammered on upside down? Only me.

My only previous carpentry experience had been constructing tree-houses with my brother King. And these had exclusively involved 4-inch nails, which bent at the third direct hit. For Jumble I had bought a massive quantity of bronze grip- fast nails, and these bent just as easily when not struck with precision.

It was after several weeks that I had to accept that saws have limited lives and simply have to be thrown away when blunt. To sharpen a saw required skill beyond my wildest imaginings, but to throw away a saw that looked perfectly good to the untrained eye was to rail against the parsimony that was the bedrock principle of the impoverished Wharram builder. The Wharram magazine- 'Sailorman' (later renamed 'Seapeople' in recognition that women are, in fact, sentient beings) was full of articles explaining how old leather shoes could be cut up to form water pump gaskets etc.

But basic woodworking law made only slow progress in my brain, in the meantime cuts and scratches would accrue, like compound interest in the Bank of Carpentry Errors, on my hands in a welter of mildly infected wounds all partially sealed in two-part glue.

And the boat had an insatiable appetite for tools. I never had enough. There was always a job that required a bigger chisel or a smaller screwdriver.

Dr. Bembridge had kindly given me the run of his toolbox, and of this I took merciless advantage. Down into the mewling mouths of the hulls went his precious hammers and spanners- all efficiently splotched with brown glue. But I was like an addict; the boat demanded more tools and engendered a new, harsher, morality in its constructor.

Clearly woodwork at school would have been far more useful than an in depth knowledge of the Dyak tribe in Borneo. By all accounts the Dyaks made pretty good dug out canoes. Occasionally I would stand on the unfinished decks of my Polynesian catamaran in its Tunbridge Wells back garden and imagine myself anchoring off the Borneo coast to see a Dyak paddle along side.

"How do you manage without two- part resorcinol glue?" I would ask.

By this stage I had been working on my own all weekend and the night would be drawing in, an hallucinatory state was easy to slip into as the brain trundled along in a kind of reverie, I could almost hear the sea and the slap of the bow wave…

Plans have to become dreams at times.

But initially, the plans that I had bought for the boat gave me a few nightmares. It was a little while before I realised that the various sheets of drawings were not always exact, and were, in fact, a bold, almost visionary, guide to construction. They were open to interpretation, like a religious text.

More fundamental mistakes could be made, and were. For instance, when I went to purchase the deck stringers from the local timber yard I presumed the measurements to be centimeters as opposed to millimeters.

Led on by blind faith I bought a huge amount of timber that was ten times too big. Back at the boat I struggled to see how these stringers would fit in a space clearly too small. Since they had cost a good half of my wood budget the reality was hard to accept. I looked at the plans, the wood, and the boat in turn, in desperate disbelief. I was nearly fourteen before I finally accepted that Father Christmas might be a mythological figure. Accepting that I had bought the wrong wood came equally hard.

With little regard for the tribulations of an ocean going (small) catamaran constructor, Sainsbury's supermarkets proposed to buy the Bembridges' house and turn it into a car park. They accepted the offer, despite my vague protestations that it was only money. Relocation, however, was not going to be easy. For a start the hulls were now much heavier and bigger.

Building the boat at the Bembridges' carried on in an evermore chaotic manner for two years. Willing volunteers would be sucked into the project, like naïve twelfth century knights onto cataclysmic Holy Land Crusades, only to leave, exhausted, after a few days. Roy, a fellow member of the Non-Violent Direct Action Group (Brighton) put his back out and took up the saxophone, and "Nutter" sawed off the end of his index finger. I carried on stalwartly.

Because two-part resorcinol glue will not set below a certain temperature, the cold of winter proved an inpenetratable barrier to further construction. Our hovel in Brighton lacked central heating and was actually colder inside than out, so I found myself continuing with the Community Programme. They had warm offices.

Emergency financing of the whole venture was also required, this time in the form of Bill Shelby and King, my brother. Bill was an old friend of mine from teacher training (we used to throw rocks at each other on Rottingdean beach by way of therapy after a day playing at being severe school teachers). Bill had the distinction of being as bad as me at playing the guitar; he was, in fact, considered bad enough to join our band 'Derek and the Gerbils', together with Noel Butterly (who emigrated to Sweden) Rufus Horne, Alan Bembridge, and me. One of our LPs was called 'Waiting for Bill' in his honour. Bill decided that he would become a 25% shareholder in Jumble, and he would pay for this privilege in the form of slave labour, and by providing a new construction site in Wimborne, Dorset.

Bill's coming saved the entire project. I showed him an old photograph of James Wharram, skinny and bespectacled on some Trinidad beach standing next to the shark like profile of a half complete boat. He looked just like Bill.

Boat moving

Bill's engineering genius soon came to the fore with the trailer he made to transport the boat, one hull at a time, to Wimborne. The chassis of two derelict Morris Minors were welded together to support a complicated cradle for the boat. The contraption was over 35 feet long, bestrewn with lighting wires and baulks of timber, and probably wholly illegal.

The only vehicle with a tow arm attached that I could borrow was Rufus's CND (Campaign For Nuclear Disarmament) Ford Transit van. He wasn't terribly keen for me to borrow it, as it would be removed from front line service in the battle against nuclear weapons. The bus was key to the operations of the NVDA, the Non-Violent-Direct-Action wing of Rufus's CND group. This usually involved long journeys to protest against, for instance, the enclosure of Common Land by the Ministry of Defence in order to site American Cruise Missiles. I convinced Rufus that, once complete, the catamaran could be used in the harassment of nuclear submarines, and, as a direct result, have an influence on ending the Cold War. This dubious argument won him over.

The usual way to move the boat was to casually invite all the people I knew to a party with free drink and "entertainment". People from Brighton would be bussed up in the CND van so that they couldn't escape. Then the small job of man handling the boat, one hull at a time, would be sprung on them.

With about 15 people each side, lifting in unison, it was possible to transport a hull. Access was through the hedge, into the neighbour's garden and up their drive to the road. Patricia was most anxious that the hedge wasn't damaged. This seemed a bit strange since the whole place was going to be flattened into a car park by Sainsburys, but people get very funny about their gardens. In the event I *had* cut down two small trees. (When the move was complete I propped them up again).

Cutting down trees went against many of my more noble instincts, but sometimes it is impossible to avoid. As a Boy Scout on camp we had coppiced two small trees in order to provide fuel to avoid starving to death. The crime was discovered and I was ceremoniously stripped of my Scout Standard in front of the entire Scout assembly. Very much like the officer who, refusing to send his men over the top in a suicide attack, is stripped of the insignias of rank before being led away to be shot. My patrol stood in silent sympathy, everyone realised that, without sufficient wood, our ordeal in a Kent wood miles from civilisation would be intolerable. Two troopers were still lying ill in the tent after failing to cook a chicken properly. I was just the scapegoat, illicit fuel scavenging was endemic, and I simply hadn't been subtle enough.

Remarkably the hull moving operation was completed with only one slipped disc. But with the Sitka Spruce mast (see later) lashed to the roof rack, and red flags flying off the rear, it seemed only too likely the police would stop us for inspection. Since the trip had to be done twice I drove in trepidation, but nothing happened! The catamaran arrived to possess the Dorset car park.

Chapter 5

TC
Catamarans

There is something delightfully sensible about a catamaran. I can imagine an ancient ancestor launching his first hollowed out log boat and, after a few capsizes, realising that if he strapped two logs together with a couple of branches then he had a far more stable craft. Better for fishing from, and with a shallow enough draft to get in really close to the shore. I bet this pivotal invention doubled the fishing potential of a human tribe and helped satiate the increased energy demands created by a larger brain.

Without a doubt the catamaran was the first sea craft to make a long voyage. One day archaeological evidence will emerge to confirm this. When 80,000 years ago the first tribe of *Homo sapiens* stared out across the narrow straits that divided Eritrea from Yemen they would have crossed on catamaran rafts. How else do you transport all the members, old and young, of a 200 strong emigrating people with all their survival tools without capsizing them?

Bizarrely there has been an immense prejudice against catamarans for many years. When, in 1876, Nathaniel Herreshoff launched a sailing catamaran to take on the monohulls of New York in the Centennial Cup regatta he won! In response the yachting establishment banned such boats from taking part in future races.

When Patrick Willis's Dad won the St.Helier Yacht Club Round The Island Race in Jersey in his 22 foot Hirondelle catamaran they did the same thing! And this was 1976!

The earliest well documented catamarans were, of course, built by the Polynesians. They used these incredibly fast craft to transit from one island to another. Huge, ocean going craft were constructed to transport migratory populations thousands of miles. The crab-claw sail remains the most efficient sail for beating upwind, the Polynesians were superb designers. They chose catamarans or proas (this has an outrigger float as opposed to a complete sister hull) because they were the only craft fast enough, or stable enough, to make feasible the vast Pacific journeys.

The Polynesians settled on the catamaran because of its enormous potential for speed and its ability to ride out the worst of the Pacific seas. A light, well-rigged catamaran will leave a monohull standing. Captain Cook was astounded at the speed of the local craft that he encountered in his explorations of the Pacific Islands. Nothing comparable existed in Europe at the time. The Polynesians built ocean-going catamarans to transfer entire viable populations to new lands like New Zealand.

The Ancient Egyptians went down the catamaran route for an entirely different reason; the catamaran's potential for ferrying huge weights. When colossal pillars needed to be floated down the Nile, two large boats would be lashed together to form a raft of unparalleled load bearing performance.

A Frenchman, Eric de Bisschop, was one of the first Westerners to be inspired by the designs of Polynesia. He undertook voyages from Hawaii to France in a catamaran based on what he had seen. But it was James Wharram who brought it all home to the UK. In 1957 he sailed his homebuilt 23ft "Tangaroa" across the Atlantic. The eye catching thing about Wharram's effort was that he did it all for about £300.

It is one of the extraordinary accidents of history that the technology of catamaran design was lost to the modern age. The idea has everything going for it; stability, speed and capacity. Obviously if a catamaran does capsize it is virtually impossible to right again, but it won't sink. If a monohull is holed it sinks like a stone due to its heavy lead or iron keel. An overturned catamaran will function as a satisfactory life-raft. There is also a misconception that catamarans have poor upwind performance compared with a monohull. In truth a decent catamaran will make progress upwind faster.

The main thing to remember with a catamaran is not to overload her. With all the extra deck space, and hull capacity, there is a tendency to pile on more and more unnecessary paraphernalia. This diminishes the cat's ability to turn "wind speed" into "hull speed through the water". Catamarans can also be over rigged. With too large a sail area the risk of capsize increases, and there is no need to over canvas. A monohull heels over in a breeze, spilling the wind. A catamaran rig remains bolt upright and the lift force from the sails accelerates the boat rather than heels it. A smaller sail area then works with much greater efficiency than the equivalent size on a monohull.

If a truly powerful gust comes along one safety feature of a cruising catamaran should be its ability to slip sideways through the water. If a catamaran is furnished with deep dagger boards, or centre plates, then these can cause the boat to trip over.

For Jumble we erected a 33ft mast, initially the Sitka Spruce mast (see later) heroically cleaved from an entire tree courtesy of Abbotts Wood in Sussex. When this later dramatically broke in the entrance to Poole harbour, in the teeth of the chain ferry, the mast was replaced by a 33ft aluminium section off a racing monohull that had broken its 45ft mast at the crosstrees. The mast came with oversized stainless steel rigging and made Jumble look quite smart. The sail at the bow, called the Yankee, was a high cut genoa that could be rolled up round the forestay via a very basic roller reefing system. An inner foresail, called the staysail, flew from half way up the mast to a strong point on the foredeck. Then there was the main sail that could be reefed smaller in the event of strong wind.

The sail complement was completed by the most glorious of all sails, the spinnaker. This lightweight massive balloon of a sail was deployed when the wind was coming from behind, and with the spinnaker up in a fresh breeze Jumble would lift her bows that few extra inches, and fly, as if in party dress, before the waves.

I did contemplate sewing the sails at home, but fortunately, talked myself out of this insanity. Arun Sails were commissioned instead and produced superb set of dacron sails. The only downside was that they required paying in real money, in advance. Twenty years later these sails were still going strong. The secret is to get them out of the sunshine as often as possible; UV destroys all fabrics, including human skin, in the end.

A cruising catamaran is a very different beast to a racing catamaran dinghy. The dinghy, like a Hobie Cat, is very easy to capsize, and not so easy to right again. A cruising cat, well designed and properly rigged, will never capsize save, perhaps, in conditions that might sink a freighter. An enemy of a fast moving cat is collision with a heavy underwater object like a tree or shipping container. These huge steel boxes are occasionally lost overboard and have the nasty habit of floating just beneath the surface due to their airtight doors. They are as good as rocks to a fast moving hull. A well designed cat will have watertight bulk heads in the forward sections of the boat; a shattering encounter with a solid object should not see the sinking of a hull.

Another worry is the breaking wave. A cat will ride out any amount of swell, as indeed will most sailing boats; it's the massive weight of water of a breaking wave that can smash a boat. Wharram's original conception involved having only slatted decks between the two hulls, with all living accommodation confined to the sides. The forward and rear decks would be spanned only by netting. The idea was that breaking seas would simply fall through the slats; also if the cat should pitch over the wind would similarly blow through. In reality a mass of water large enough will not pass through a slatted deck quick enough to prevent it acting like a solid sheet. Cats that have used webbing instead of netting have discovered this problem too. The webbing simply has too much surface area.

Obviously a slatted deck also allows the odd rogue wave to periodically soak the crew. This is why crew members on a Wharram often dress as if recently rescued from some maritime disaster. Indeed the whole boat may resemble a raft fitted out with emergency sails.

All Wharrams, however devoted in the original years to an unadulterated design, end up by boarding-over all, or at least part, of the deck slats. Jumble was no exception. The best defence against breaking waves remains firstly to avoid them, and secondly to have a vessel strong enough to withstand them.

Once you have begun the process of boarding over the slatted decks you do begin to wonder why the hell you are trying to live in the claustrophobically tiny compartments provided by the narrow V-shaped hulls, when it might have been possible to have a decent sized enclosed space between the hulls! This is an heretical thought in Wharram circles. Comfort, shelter? Are you crazy? In fact in later designs even Wharram began to crack, and on the bigger 42ft boats tiny cabins made an appearance where a wet and exhausted crewman might take shelter from the elements. And possibly where they might even snatch a few moments of sleep.

On Jumble we eventually constructed a small triangle pod that an adult could just sit upright in. It was lashed on and could be quickly removed if James Wharram should turn up for a snap inspection.

James Wharram may have been influenced by Polynesian design, but not all their techniques translated so well. Your average Polynesian boat was constructed from the materials at hand. Wood and vegetable based lashings. They had no iron. As a result the boats unavoidably had a good deal of flex. The hulls could twist and turn slightly in relation to each other. This may have been a good thing when you had a very lightweight boat that was frequently beached to have the lashings tightened. When you have larger hulls made from marine ply that can weigh a good ton or more each, the idea of having flexible beam mounts is not an unparalleled success. The trouble begins when a little bit of "give" in the lashings holding the beams to the deck, stretches by small increments to become a lot of "give" and the beams work loose. On some designs Wharram had the crossbeams holding the two hulls together fastened down on blocks of rubber. On Jumble we abandoned this idea in favour of beams set in immovable troughs bolted to the boat. This setup allowed for no flexing. The only handicap was the fact that the beam troughs could quite easily fill with water and become rot traps. Drainage holes were drilled in a bid to prevent this future disaster, and lethal quantities of anti-life chemicals were drenched into the wood.

Obviously the beams holding the two hulls of a catamaran together are of the utmost importance. If they fail, or become detached, you are in thick yoghurt.

But just like our Polynesian antecedents, poverty dictated the most economic solution. Elegant hardwood laminates were spurned in favour of great planks of "eight by two" stuck together. These were dropped into the wooden troughs. Well, they were lined up and then sledge hammered home with increasing desperation. With the kitty empty stainless steel bolts were replaced with galvanized ones coated in bituminous epoxy. But the final result seemed strong enough and Jumble proved a very stiff boat. "Stiff", in boating parlance, means unflexing, not yielding and solid in the face the sea's slaps. A bit like a boxer on pain killers.

Every so often one reads in the yachting press of a catamaran foundering. Occasionally the crossbeams of some homebuilt giant cat have simply rotted, lost all strength and given way. Once excessive movement has begun then, in a big sea, the boat will simply twist and convulse its way to destruction. There is a school of thought that claims that no cruising cat has capsized under bare poles, but maybe the crew subject to this calamity have never lived to report the event!

We read about various ideas people had mooted for preventing or remedying a capsize. Large automatic inflating devices could be installed. Indeed on top of some dinghy catamarans a torpedo shaped flotation bulb is bolted to the top of the mast. But these would be large and unwieldy to place on a cruising cat, and the drag penalty would in itself be potentially dangerous.

On Jumble we always came back to the hope that she was impossible to over canvas, and that her centre-plateless, V-shaped hulls would side slip *in extremis* rather than dig in and precipitate a capsize.

Wharram Catamarans

James Wharram, a charismatic Englishman, built and sailed a wooden catamaran back in the 1960's. His early experiments spawned a host of similar catamarans, all known as Wharrams and all sharing some bizarre idiosyncrasies.

Wharram loves catamarans, especially ones that have some sort of Polynesian influence. This Polynesian influence is difficult to exactly pinpoint but it has something to do with windswept decks, scantily clad women and men, and a lot of rope lashings. These sorts of boats were unfairly represented according to James.

His designs caught the imagination of many people, and a good number of them bought plans of the Tane Nui, Tangaroa or Tiki and discovered that a good imagination was a truly vital component of the boat building project. You had to imagine that a completed boat was possible despite the desperate hardships of the solo boat builder.

The hull shape of all early Wharrams was a severe V. The side profile was a delightful banana curve, which, if extended, would eventually form a complete circle.

Wharram's philosophy was that a catamaran should not carry enough sail area to jeopardize its stability, masts should remain relatively short and lee-boards used only with caution, if at all. An extension of this idea was that the deck area between the hulls should remain clear, with, as mentioned before, slatted decks allowing clear passage for wind and waves.

Many hundreds of people have embarked on the Wharram self builds. To begin this adventure is to become inveigled into an intriguing subculture that has survived, little changed, from the 1960's. Self-sufficiency, free love, the call of the sea and the virtues of the West Epoxy Resin System for gluing together marine ply joints, are the holy tenets of this way of life.

A similar group of people was inspired by Thor Hyerdahl's ocean crossings in reed boats. There was a magic about the simplicity of these ancient sea craft, the merits of their historical accuracy were incidental, and what mattered was encountering the ocean full on without too much technology to mute the experience.

Probably the single most attractive part of the Wharram design is its economy; the plans provide an apparent blueprint for even the most desperately poor persons to equip themselves with an ocean going vessel. All you needed was time, wood and ...epoxy resin. For many it was the only option. It was for me.

Sadly the dreams of foreign ports, encounters with exotic Pacific peoples, remote sheltered anchorages beneath swaying coconuts, often remain exactly that. Dreams. The reality of building a boat from scratch on a shoestring budget is usually overwhelming. People begin and fail at the first few hurdles.

First you need a place to build. Ideally a watertight heated shed, or at least some sort of Poly-tunnel. And you may not need this space for months, but for years. There is only so much one person can do in a day. Even a skilled carpenter, with good power tools, can take a good while to construct just one hull frame.

In 1987 I went looking, out of curiosity, for a semi complete Wharram project to take over. I found a wide, wonderful and often rather melancholy collection of boats in fields, back gardens, mud flats and sheds. Some had been encapsulated by the homes they adjoined, some were already in advanced states of decay, a few had been on the go for decades, and none looked like they were ever going to see the sea.

Max, in his mid 50's, showed me his Narai Mk. III Wharram catamaran. He had begun building in 1978 and he still lived in the temporary caravan parked in the same field as the boat, marooned in a crop of turnips. He hobbled around, the damp had got to his joints, and he showed us with pride his novel departure from the original Wharram plans. (Nearly all Wharram builders feel the need to improve the plans - sometimes with disastrous consequences). Max had built the crossbeams that hold the two hulls together from mild steel. He had welded great lengths in a bizarre criss-cross matrix, a little like a miniature Forth Road Bridge. My mouth fell open at this immense superstructure, already beginning to rust, but I felt duty bound to praise his efforts. The man had clearly lost the plot. For a little while I walked around the unturned hulls in the drizzle before retreating to his caravan for coffee. His wife, Sue, brought out a photograph album documenting the boat's progress through the years.

There, on page one was a much younger looking Max, stripped to the waist and sawing a large sheet of marine ply. And there was Sue, looking rather fetching in rubber gloves, clearly mixing glue. The initial few pages of photographs were optimistically captioned with things like,"Max puts the final nail in hatch cover number one! Only 9 to go!"

You could almost smell the beckoning ocean. But the years went by and as the frames get built, the deck goes on, one cabin goes up, and the photographs get more episodic. The captions became less numerous, and none humorous. Then in 1984 there is a hiatus for two years. I ask why, and am told by Sue, "Ah, yes, well Max had a bit of a breakdown. Had to take a break. And I, well, I developed an allergic intolerance to epoxy. Couldn't fillet a joint even dressed as a spaceman."

Things hadn't progressed much since. Max's welding course, presumably part of his occupational therapy, had resulted in the hopelessly elaborate and heavy steel crossbeams. But they would clearly sink the boat. Obviously they had finally realised that the dream had slipped through their fingers. And what remained was up for sale.

Chapter 6

TC
Wimborne 1987

Once off loaded from the home made low loaders the hulls were installed in a car park in Wimborne, Dorset. This was a fairly audacious act since Wimborne was a genteel market town, not used to having town centre car parks hijacked by catamaran builders. But somehow this car park was the centre of a drawn out planning case, the council owned it and wanted to put a road through it but repeatedly ran out of funds to actually undertake the work. The result was an abandoned six-bedroom house which was squatted in by Bill and his brother, and a car park with several garages which was similarly commandeered by the Sherrit brothers.

Rooms were full of junk; one room was entirely full of car parts including about 20 batteries all in various states of discharge.

This situation had persisted for several years and the Wharram was just another large article in a car park that boasted three Morris Minor vans (Bills favourite vehicle), several A30's (Bill's brother's favourite vehicle), an Enterprise dinghy, assorted engine blocks, piles of wood and detritus of squatting life.

There proved no need to rebuild the extensive polythene city that had so tormented Particia Bembridge since one of the garages was tall enough and long enough to accommodate a hull. This provided a luxurious building environment, enough to turn us soft. Only the spartan, freezing cold, desolation of the squat kept us hardened. The Wimborne squat was one of those damp buildings that are actually colder inside than outside. In his room Bill had discovered a fireplace and would light great blazes using, on occasion, the very door frames to fuel the flames.

The kitchen, although one of the smaller rooms, was filled to the brim with unwashed articles. It remains one of the most unhygienic places I have ever visited – save, perhaps, some French toilets. There seemed to exist an undeclared biological war between the members of the squat.

Various items that had been used and then disowned were simply left to gather mould.

There were about four of them, all out to poison one another.

One squat member, Brian, I never saw. He lived a nocturnal existence like a rare bat. The door to his room remained closed and Bill infrequently sighted him, occasionally flitting to the toilet, or returning with curried take-aways. For me, during the entire boat build, Brian made no physical appearance. But as a ghost in the squat I was always eerily aware of him, watching, monitoring, and raiding the fridge. Bill had a separate, padlocked, fridge in his room; actually in this paranoid squat everyone had a secure fridge in their room. Vanessa, a psychiatric auxiliary night nurse, and Bill's brother's sometime girlfriend had a fridge freezer and a violent temper, inflamed beyond reason by alcohol.

But the great benefit of the whole set up was that it was free, an essential necessity for the very poor boat builder. At this time I came into possession of a Peugeot 505 family estate in shockingly bad condition. Known as the African Taxi the Peugeot 505 was a bit like a Lancaster bomber; able to absorb a tremendous amount of punishment before going down. This car also happened to be the longest estate car in Western Europe and, inspired by the Sherrit brothers, I soon had three of them all parked nose to tail down the Brighton street where I lived. Two were cannibalised to keep the third on the road. This was 1985 and must have been the last time that it was possible to undertake this kind of derelict vehicle display on a public road in a town.

With a roof rack the 505 could transport phenomenal quantities of building materials and, as I was soon to discover, children, prams, bikes etc. It was also considerably quicker than hitching. Apart from a stubborn radiator leak, no operable starting motor (which necessitated parking on a hill) and the need to avoid second gear, it was a fine, if rusty, friend. In this machine I commuted from Brighton to Wimborne.

And so the construction of the catamaran proceeded. Local townspeople would wander in to see how things were going; we became minor celebrities. The cabin tops were screwed on. And it was at this stage when we realised that internal space was not generous on this kind of Wharram. We also discovered that all marine necessities from anchors to stainless steel bolts were staggeringly expensive. Our salvation was a kind of marine auction held regularly in nearby Poole, and marine jumbles. Everything was obtained from these sources, and if it didn't fit, Bill had ways of making it fit.

Yet even with two of us slaving at construction, desperation sometimes afflicted us. Poverty and cold sometimes lead to boat builders being gripped by a kind of Sartrean hopelessness. Bill and I were beginning to fall to this disease when, just in time, King and Patrick arrived to new infusions of just as senseless enthusiasm. They brought much needed money and labour to the project. Once again I could envisage the bow wave, the sun on the horizon and all the other associated delusions that keep a Wharram builder slaving away at about 10p an hour.

Patrick was a friend of mine from school who always had a soft spot for crazy ideas. We shared an innate inability to comprehend German, coming equal last in the German language examination in 1975. Having nearly been expelled from school for begging outside a bank in Jersey's capital, St. Helier, Patrick went on to become a surveyor. But not before becoming sucked into the seedy world of catamaran construction.
Gradually the boat took shape, but not without some setbacks. The cold winter of 1986, the absence of a sensible heating system and dietary impoverishment frequently sapped Bill's strength. His manic working habits sometimes faltered as he lay shivering in bed.

When Bill's girlfriend, and later wife, Susan, was enamoured enough of the venture to purchase 50% of Jumble, together with my brother King, and then Patrick (also committed to 50% each à la 'The Producers') it was possible to keep the whole show on the road. Other desperate measures became necessary as the expense of fatherhood, let alone boat ownership, finally dawned on me.

So, on the strength of having been to Poland, and being able to count to 10 in German, I decided to go for an interview as a tour guide taking groups of Americans to Russia. We hopefuls were gathered in a room in London where first we had to display fluency in two languages. Not one, but two. As the person next to me rabbitted on about the nuances of the complex French novel he had just read, I wracked my brains for something to say in French. When it was finally my go, I came up with "J'habite dans un grand maison avec ma famile" all coming out like a three year old. In German all I could manage was "Ein, dvie, trie.." up to ten, but it was said with such great gusto that I got a round of applause, and the job.

Making Money – (roubles)

My first assignment as a tour director with EF was to Soviet Era Moscow and Leningrad. The tour group arrived from the States and landed first at Copenhagen, Denmark. I was dispatched there to meet them in my crispy new EF sweatshirt and matching cardigan.

A large, exhausted looking man lurched through the arrivals door. He surveyed the hall as if in search of someone to kill. I rather hesitantly held up my welcome to Europe EF sign, and he stalked towards me.

"You work for EEE F?" he asked, gently swaying as he perspired. I wasn't entirely convinced of the probity of admitting this. As I stuttered he jabbed a finger at my incriminating EF Tour Director badge.

"You work for EEE F!" he exclaimed, emphasising the E and the F as if they were hideously blasphemous.

"Welcome to Europe," I proposed,

"Welcome fuck," he retorted, "I'm going to sue EEE F, I'm going to sue you, I'm going to sue you personally, I'm going to sue your mother and father and any pets you may have…"

Things weren't going well, especially as I was relying on a large tip to supplement my very low basic EF wage. A dissolute group of hollow eyed American teenagers and their teachers had gathered round.

"Is this Russia?" one asked.

"Can we go to our hotel now?" another pleaded.

Their angry leader, whose lapel badge declared him to be Gary S. Benson, stepped up close to me and continued his diatribe,

"Do you know how long we have been travelling to get this far?"

"Twelve hours?" I guessed out of politeness.

"WRONG! – twenty seven hours, twenty seven miserable hours cooped up like so many battery chickens to get this far, and all thanks to fucking EEE F!"

Apparently, to save money, EF tried to amalgamate groups, and route them the cheapest possible way across the Atlantic. Evidently this group had been shuttled around the States for quite a bit before finally arriving here. They seemed to have left Chicago and visited Boston, Atlanta, Philadelphia and New York. They weren't happy.

Lack of sleep had rendered them a little hysterical. When I advised the group that the flight to Leningrad was delayed for two hours there was a universal groan. People slumped down over their hand luggage, there were tears. Gary shook his head in rapid little jerks; he looked dangerously close to a breakdown. But worse was to follow.

When we arrived in Leningrad the luggage failed to arrive with us. Nobody could tell me where it might be or when it might arrive. We left the airport to board a coach driven by a very disconsolate driver called Nicholas. He had been waiting for us in the freezing cold for hours and he, like everyone else, considered that the blame lay with me. Also on board was Frieda, our wizen, sour-faced Intourist guide. She didn't even smile when I gave her the customary bribe of two hundred Benson and Hedges. My shivering group scraped some of the ice from the inside of the windows with their credit cards.

"There is a temporary problem with the heating system," explained Frieda.

By some bizarre turn of events we were booked into one of the finest hotels in Leningrad. Our rooms commanded wonderful views over the river and of the battleships whose guns had signalled the start of the Bolshevik Revolution. All this meant little to the comatosed Americans who retired immediately to their rooms.

Only I turned up for dinner in the banqueting hall, plates of caviar and smoked salmon stretched down the table into the distance. It was a terrible waste. What would Lenin have thought, or Trotsky? My last teacher at primary school had been obsessed with the Russian

Revolution; his name was, appropriately enough, Mr. Marx. We all had to write an exhaustive project on the Bolsheviks, not that Mr. Marx was a communist; he was a solid conservative who, for instance, considered Cliff Richard's jazzed up rendition of an old hymn an outrageous heresy. The main thing I remembered about the 1917 revolt and its consequences for the world was that Trotsky was assassinated in Mexico with an ice axe. I had spent a lot of time on a graphic illustration of this bloody event.

The waiter appeared with bottles of Russian champagne, I tried to explain my group's absence,

"They're all asleep. Long journey, very tired."

He looked at me strangely and then furtively asked,

"You have dollars?"

It was 1986 and the beginning of the end for the Iron Curtain.

The following morning the schedule demanded an impossibly optimistic 6 a.m. breakfast followed by a tour of the city. Only a handful made it onto the coach, which was still piloted by the sullen Nicholas, and compered by the grim fairy Frieda. She explained that she was going to the airport to see if she could locate our luggage, and I was left to conduct the tour of Peter The Great's personal city. As such the tour was a little bland, and lacking, almost entirely, in specific details,

"And here in front of us again is…a river. A great wide river, not unlike the Volga."

"And here now opens up a grand avenue, tree lined and leading up to a…big building, a big building with lots of windows that could have been a palace. Probably was a palace in fact!"

"This may well have been a point where, in the 1917, the Bolshevik peasants gathered to storm the Romanov Winter Palace which could have been, now I think about it, that building back there".

Gary, the large group leader, sat at the front of the coach and listened to me with only mild interest. He was probably still in shock. My heroic efforts on the tannoy probably washed over him, and I think he was a little sheepish about his behaviour at the airport. To impress him I tried out my one sentence of Russian on the driver, this elicited a torrent of incomprehensible Russian from Nicholas, complete with gesticulations and grimaces. I smiled, looked back at the passengers and realised they were expecting me to continue with the conversation. Foolishly, in retrospect, I took the gamble that no one else on the coach understood any Russian at all and engaged Nicholas in a long-winded sentence of entirely fictitious pidgin Russian.

Naturally he replied that he had no idea what I was going on about and turned back to his wheel in disgust.

"He says he's overworked and underpaid," I explained to the passengers. They seemed duly convinced and impressed at my linguistic prowess, a minor deceit that caused me a lot of bother later.

Two days later, just before we were due to catch the night train from Leningrad to Moscow, the luggage turned up and spirits rose. I read up on the history of Moscow in the minutes I had to myself, and by the time we arrived at our new hotel I was more confident.

The onerous schedule demanded that the tour guide take his party on an introductory visit to the famous Moscow underground. Our hotel lay within a short walk of one of the out-lying subway stations; these extensions had been largely excavated by German prisoners of war. This fact was largely glossed over by Intourist, they preferred to emphasise the astonishing punctuality of the Moscow underground system. And in this they were correct. Trains stopped for a maximum of thirty seconds at each station and then departed regardless. I dutifully studied my subway map and ushered the Americans on board the first train heading for the city centre. We made rapid progress and changed onto a new line. The stations became ever more fabulous in their design; they were quite captivating and in a short time I realised I had lost track of where we were. The problem was compounded by the fact that the station names were written in Cyrillic, which could have been Martian for all I knew. I desperately tried to transcribe the strange markings with similar station names on my map. This all had to be done in the few seconds allowed at each stop, whilst simultaneously trying to look calm and totally sure of my position. After an hour the Americans began asking awkward questions about how long to go, and where were we in relation to the hotel.

I had begun to flush hot and cold when, by sheer luck, I identified the station we had just halted at on the map. It was a remote satellite stop of the Moscow underground. But I knew where we were and by concentrating like a demon I navigated a return route.

At the end of a week I had learned a few basic Russian phrases, principally to do with finding out where I was. It had been an exhausting way of earning money. When the group and I turned up at Moscow airport to fly back to the West I was keen to abandon them forever. But Gary had one more sting in his tail. When, at the check-in, I asked him for the passports, he turned pale.

"I've left them in the hotel safe."

"You've left them in the hotel safe!"

"Yes".

My mind went into overdrive. There must be a way to resolve this; it was still two hours before take off.

"OK Gary, you and I will grab a taxi back to the city. There will be just time to get the passports and return."

I turned to go, but Gary held me back by the shoulder. He looked unusually sheepish,

"They're not in the hotel safe in Moscow, I left them in Leningrad".

Delinquents

I obtained a job as a youth worker at a drop-in centre for the children of a rather monotonous run down council estate. Burnt out cars regularly occupied parking bays just outside the fortified building and groups of disaffected teenagers intimidated old people as they attempted entry to the local shop nearby.

This was an armoured shop; windows had been replaced by zinc plates originally embellished with a mural of a shop window. They had long been obliterated by artless local graffiti.

I was warned not to leave my bike outside; instead it was locked away in a broom cupboard. My job, it soon transpired, was to supervise the use of the amenities; these consisted of a pool table and a stereo system. Any unsupervised equipment would be promptly removed and destroyed. If it was too difficult to remove it would be destroyed *in situ*. The pool table was a popular pastime, but left unattended, the green baize would be ripped and the cues snapped. There had been other exotic amenities, but these were ancient memories. Like the table football game. This, ironically, was fondly recalled by the local lads, yet it was they who ripped the wooden players from their mounts and trampled them to obliteration.

The devastated remains still lent up against the hall wall. An icon to a lost Eden.

It was a case of the dogs biting the hand that feeds them, or in this case, semi-deprived teenagers sabotaging the means of their own entertainment.

Nonetheless, the facility was operated by young social workers of unbounded optimism. Sharon, the supervisor, smiled on in the face of repeated failure in her attempts to alleviate deprivation. Malcolm, the caretaker, saw his role in more military terms. His was a battle against the forces of Evil. In an ideal world he would have barricaded the whole place, dug trenches and used all necessary force to defend his Kingdom. It was a fairly realistic attitude, born out of several years in the front line against vandalism. Sharon was not so jaded; she was innocent and recently qualified with a social work university degree. Sharon and Malcolm had an uneasy working relationship. She was pushing back the boundaries of civilization; he was fighting for its very survival. My early naivety placed me in Sharon's camp, at least briefly.

Using my emerging boat building skills I embarked upon a skate board ramp building project. Some of the lads joined in and found good homes for several hammers, screw drivers and other tools. Others found time, late one night, to drag the virtually complete ramp to the car park where they attempted to mount it with a stolen Peugeot before torching both car and ramp for good measure. This incident, together with the theft of my bike from the broom cupboard, left me a little cynical about what might be achieved.

Our local office, like First World War generals planning yet another offensive, decided to take a group of these kids on a camping trip to the South of France. A minibus was reserved, a group of eight teenagers recruited, and Sharon was designated Leader, with Dianna, the office secretary, as The Helper. The ferry was booked before it was realised that neither Sharon nor Dianna could drive. I was implored to join this happy ten day excursion as The Driver.

It was a terrible mistake.

Initially I was lulled into a false sense of security; a rough crossing on the ferry had rendered most of the group sea-sick. Early efforts to drink stolen duty free gin were regurgitated, and so we disembarked at Dieppe with everyone sober and relatively biddable. But the return of land legs saw the return of unacceptable behaviour.

Firstly Kevin and Damien lit up cigarettes just behind me,

"Sorry lads but you can't smoke in the van," I said.

"But I've gotta have a fag mate," retorted Kevin.

"You will have to wait til we stop," I reiterated.

"I can't fuckin' wait," insisted Kevin.

Sharon feebly suggested we make a fag stop every half hour or so. It was the beginning of the slide to anarchy.

We made slow progress towards the south; fag stops, toilet stops, and car-sickness stops punctuated the journey. Occasional squabbles elicited death threats. We arrived at a campsite tired and disconsolate, but our troubles were not yet over. In the few hours before dark some of the lads contrived to borrow, and then sink, several of the small punts that the campsite rented out on an adjoining pond.

The campsite owner was apoplectic with fury, he wanted us to leave "immediatement", and it was only with my abject apologies, our entire entertainment fund and Sharon's copious tears that we were allowed to stay for one night only.

It was fairly easy to identify which children had sunk the boats since they were soaking wet. They denied all knowledge, claiming that the "fuckin' frogs" had framed them. In the morning we left as early as possible.

Within half an hour Kevin decided to light up a fag in the back.

"I think you should put that cigarette out, Kevin," said Sharon.

"I think you should shut up," replied Kevin.

Sharon sat in miserable silence; tears welled up in her eyes. Diana, The Helper, intensely examined the contents of her handbag; Kevin took a big drag on the fag and blew the smoke towards the front of the van. Emboldened, Michael produced a pack of Gaulloises with a flourish, and placed one in his mouth and lit up. A foul stench permeated the atmosphere.

This was too much. I slid over to the side of the road and slammed on the brakes: the transit screeched to an abrupt halt.

"Right, everyone out!" I yelled.

Once alongside the road I locked the doors and waved the van keys in the air,

"We are 800 kilometers from home, I am your only hope of getting either to or from the South of France", I explained, and then threw the keys dramatically on the ground. There was a subdued silence. I stood on the keys and tried to look as crazy as possible. Even Sharon and Diana shuffled awkwardly from foot to foot.

"These are the rules", I continued Moses-like, "You will not smoke in the van; you will not damage any property; you will not drink any alcohol. If anyone disagrees with me, or threatens me then I'm not driving. We are going to enjoy this holiday and you will behave yourselves."

There was murmured assent and we eventually embarked, this time in a stilted atmosphere of suppressed ill-will. Order, however, was maintained. Although the first campsite we attempted to populate near the beach turned us away (having received warning of a wild group of

English schoolchildren), the second allowed us in. Kevin and Damien, both somewhat larger than me, eyed me with those slit eyes of barely controlled hatred. But they didn't smoke in the van.

Enforcing a curfew of 11 p.m., reasonable language and relative sobriety took its toll. I had to maintain the relentless image of a virtual psychopath on the edge of violence to underpin my control. I realised that at the first sign of weakness I would be savaged by the pack.

As a result the kids had a fairly good holiday, they learnt to surf and cook pork chops on the barbeque; but the change was only skin deep. On the way home they became evermore brazen with each passing kilometer. It became evident that once back in Brighton Kevin was going to exact his revenge; as a result I dropped him off first. With his absence Damien wasn't quite as bold, but I dropped him off next nonetheless. The others were deposited back at their various homes in order of size and belligerence.

I handed in my notice the next day. I was resolved to carry on with boat building with greater vigour. The escape from Western 'Civilisation' had become even more important.

Chapter 7

TC
Jumble build style (Sea-Rover)

As the hulls took form the boat reminded me of a series 3 Land Rover; uncompromisingly utilitarian, slightly over-engineered. She might have a fine Polynesian curve to her hull but the rest, especially the cabins, were, to put it mildly, rugged.

The cabin windows were a case in point. Small oblongs of Perspex about one foot by six inches, they were bolted on with a gasket of Sikaflex using at least sixty stainless steel bolts. There was a distinct Soviet spaceship feel about them; functional, brutal, and with no compromise made regarding aesthetics. Their design was wholly inspired by an article I had read in Sea People about the trials and tribulations of a Wharram builder whose windows had leaked. He had taken them out and re-bedded them. They still leaked. He took them out, added more bolts, re-bedded them and still they leaked. Finally he took them out, reduced the window size, and placed a bolt every three centimeters. This worked. I took this agonising account of much labour to heart and decided to have windows that would never leak from day one. The result was Ilushnikov oblong windows barely big enough to see out of and clamped home with many, many bolts.

The rest of the boat was built with similar Cold War strategy. Basically the question was asked, "Would this part of the boat survive within 10 miles of a tactical nuclear exchange?"
If Bill or I had our doubts then some heavy duty hot galvanised steel fitting or similar would be installed to make sure.

I think Bill acquired this construction mentality from Morris Minor repairs. These were always oversized and over strength, a consequence of Bill's liberal amateur welding style and fear of having to re-weld a floor-pan again in the future. The boat was overbuilt as a result, and a little heavier than necessary. Not a good thing for a catamaran which relies on comparative lightness for its performance.

A Wharram catamaran is built like a skeleton. Ribs protrude up from a curved spine and the skin of marine ply is glued and screwed on. Epoxy resin is the adhesive of choice. But it comes at a price: it is a volatile cocktail of chemicals. Human beings soon become allergic to the touch of it. One of my friends, Ozzie Haines, became hyper sensitive to it; even a brief close encounter would see him erupt in hideous skin boils. The only way is to dress up like a spaceman, and wear thick gloves and breathing apparatus.

This naturally conflicts with the happy-go-lucky, as-naked-as-possible, clothing preferences of your average Wharram builder. Only too often "epoxy intolerance" would be quoted as the reason for abandoning a life's work.

The other vicious quality of epoxy resin was its temperamental approach to setting. That is solidifying as glue. Sometimes it would not. Sometimes it would remain an unhandleable gooey mess, perhaps for months. Maybe there had been too much moisture in the air, or the temperature had dipped too low, or the chemicals were just a little too old. We employed epoxy resin only in the final stages of the build. The huge vats of resorcinol glue that came with the semi complete hulls sufficed for most of the work.

Sometimes problems would not surface until a late stage in construction, and the hapless builder would discover he had spent thousands of hours on a boat with the strength of a stack of cards.

The other, somewhat speedier, aspect to go wrong was to see the epoxy set spectacularly quickly. The newly mixed resin would gurgle like a witch's broth, become explosively hot, issue forth poisonous fumes and then set forever, entombing all brushes, in a grotesque block. These problems were not fully explored in the plans issued by the designer, James Wharram. He probably had his eye on different horizons.

Susan and Bill

When I first met Bill he was living in tiny cottage in the high street of Rottingdean, a small village on the Sussex coast. The cottage had been built when people were not fed well enough to grow taller than 5ft; the ceilings were low and the doorways even lower. Bill was about 6ft so the place was a considerable inconvenience, but that was all he could afford.

I popped round to visit him one afternoon and there in the front room was Susan. She was sitting in front of the fire holding a bloodstained towel to her mouth. Apparently she had been out cycling with Bill and had come off after a brake failure and knocked out her front two teeth on the curb.

"This is Tim Susan…show him your teeth".

Susan dropped the towel and smiled toothlessly,

"awowow im," she said politely.

I thought this showed great forbearance in the face of adversity. This attribute was to prove very important in the years to come.

"We've booked to see a dentist tomorrow morning", Bill told me as if this were a special treat, like going to the cinema.

Susan was a biochemist and had a proper job in the pathology laboratory of a hospital. Bill, who was doing a Post Graduate Certificate in Education, had met her at Bath University. She was a tall woman who had the unusual trait of stating exactly what was on her mind, regardless of the feelings of others. Once you realised she meant no harm it was actually quite an amusing mannerism.

When she and Bill got together she incorporated Morris Minor Travellers into her lifestyle with good grace. I think she initially thought that Bill's obsession with this type of car and steam engines would pass.

When Bill joined the Wharram building syndicate it was only a matter of time before she too was sucked into its deadly vortex. Her ownership of a sewing machine condemned her to many evenings of virtual slavery constructing waterproof covers for the bunk bed foam cushions. Her bank balance was, of course, heartlessly exploited.

Bill's genius lay with improvisation. He could, and would, attempt all things practical from welding, to gas connections, to high voltage electrical work; and all this regardless of professional knowledge or innate skill. Nothing was too dangerous. He was a big bloke with immense hands and fingernails like wide screw drivers. Shortsighted he wore round wire framed glasses that were inevitably flecked with paint and oil. He was possessed of a demonic energy that forced him to rush from one glorious half-finished project to another until exhaustion floored him.

When we could find no suitably robust pintels to hang the rudders on, Bill manufactured some from mild steel, rushing up and down the stairs to heat them in his bedroom fire. It was this practical response to all the various problems facing a boat builder that kept the show on the road. It was not without consequences. He was also trying to become a teacher, and after a particularly stressful day in a classroom, he failed to notice that the lorry ahead had stopped. The Morris smashed into the tailgate at about 40 mph. Bill survived because he was wearing his safety belt, but repairs to the Morris seriously damaged the Wharram building timetable.

The Sitka Spruce Mast

The Forestry Commission agreed to sell me, to my immense surprise, three full grown Sitka Spruce trees located in Abbotts Wood, near Lewes. All I had to do was locate them, cut them down and transport them home.

I had written to the Forestry Commission as a wild stab in the dark. My idea was to stay close to nature, and cheap. In retrospect it would have been far less expensive and quicker to buy a second hand aluminium mast, but inexperience led me down the whole tree route.

I had already invested in an adze, a kind of sideways axe, medieval in character, and rather dangerous in action. The local Do-It-Yourself store had ordered for me specially; it was the first adze they had ever procured. The shop owner been rather surprised to find one listed in a vast tool supplier manual. With this instrument I intended to trim a Sitka spruce tree into a superb mast.

This was not as easy as I hoped.

First, finding the trees themselves was no easy task. Although the Forestry Commission man had kindly issued me with a map, it was not that exact. This was compounded by the fact that I did not know how a Sitka spruce differed from the various other pine trees growing in the vicinity. I had set my heart on a Sitka because the Wharram build magazine declared them to be the only tree worth considering for masts. I abandoned my Dad's VW Beetle on the outskirts of the wood and wandered haphazardly through the trees.

With a small copy of "A guide to trees" open in one hand, I finally located the stand of Sitka circled in red on the Forestry Commission man's map. Sitka spruces are strong, durable, flexible but light. The superlatives expressed in books were persuasive, but in reality how on earth do you assess a tree's height? I wandered round and round trees till I felt quite dizzy, for the life of me I couldn't tell if a particular tree was straight or possessed of a slight curve. In the end I picked out three likely candidates for execution and marked them out with purple crosses of chalk.

Now I addressed myself to the problem of cutting down the trees and extracting them from the forest. Even I realised that lashing a 40ft spruce to the top of a VW Beetle would end in tears. I grudgingly accepted that I would need to seek help. Back in Brighton I rang Alan whose small advert in the local free paper declared he was capable of any job,

"Nothing Too Large or Too Small". It was this claim of coping with the "Too Large" that encouraged me. When I met him he confided in me that he had only recently started up in business and I was his first commission. He had a chain saw and a Landrover pick-up, which was a good thing, but he had never cut down or transported a tree, which was a bad thing. His initial optimism was as unbounded as mine however, and he got the job.

The next weekend we met up in Abbotts Wood. Alan had convinced a friend of his with a removals van to turn up to transport the trees back to Brighton. This promptly stuck in the mud of the forest track and had to be winched out with Alan's Landrover. Its driver and owner, Gerry, lost his nerve at this point and indicated that he was intending to return home,

"I didn't think you meant real trees," he moaned to Alan.

They had a brief altercation before Gerry agreed to stay. I wasn't sure what Alan had said but Gerry looked quite pale when we trooped into the wood as if on an SAS mission with the chainsaw slung over Alan's shoulder like a machine gun.

The rain of the previous two days had rendered the ground muddy, and it took me some time to realise that the marked trees had been washed clean. By this time Alan was in a foul mood. In desperation I pointed to a likely Spruce and Alan set to with the chainsaw. The tree shortly crashed down through the undergrowth with a hissing rumble. I walked up to fallen giant feeling like a murderer and attempted to roll it. I thought this would soon tell me if it were straight or not. It was impossible to budge, even with three of us straining. The tree weighed far more than I had remotely conceived.

I stared down its length; I could clearly discern a curve.

"Sorry Alan, I think we might have to go for another one", I said.

Alan just raised his eyebrows in reply. About 45 minutes later we had cut down about six trees, all were either too short or bent.

I felt like a serial murderer of trees.

"Do you actually have any fucking idea what kind of fucking tree you want?" asked Alan. Gerry stood next to him evermore disconsolately.

"I'll never get 'em in my van", he muttered.

I was beginning to sweat in desperation.

"This one looks perfect!" I exclaimed.

In the end we claimed three trees from the wood. Alan reversed his Landrover as close as he dared and we hauled the spruce out using chains. Gerry's van visibly groaned under the weight and the trees stuck out about eight-foot at the back. It was all horribly illegal and Gerry's price had inflated to £30. Back in Brighton I persuaded my house mates to man-handle the trees into the back garden.

"I'll have them finished and out of here inside of 3 months!" I declared.

In my dreams!

Adzing was a desperately hard process. I adzed day and night. I adzed till I grew great calluses on my hands. I adzed till I hated the adze.

Sure enough the masts took shape, never quite straight and then, to my horror, as the wood dried out, long cracks appeared. I poured linseed oil into these until the whole garden was permeated with the smell. It was a grim business. But the boat finally got a wooden, slightly curved, spruce mast.

Chapter 8

TC
The Mission

There was a boy in my class at school called Robert Le Cras whose father built a large wooden motor boat in his back garden. When, after several years, it was launched the vessel floated awkwardly; stern down or something similar. Mr. Le Cras, evidently a perfectionist, hated it. He beached the vessel and hacked it up with a chainsaw.

I was amazed when I heard this, couldn't he have just retrimmed it, added some ballast or whatever? But no, he felt compelled to destroy it. Now, having built a boat, I can understand where he was coming from. The boat had become so all-consuming that it had sidelined the rest of his life. He wanted his revenge. I suspect that he would have sawn it up regardless of how it floated. Frankenstein was similarly overcome when his creature turned into a monster as soon as he imbued it with life.

I had some distinct advantages over Mr. Le Cras and Frankenstein: Firstly, I was almost the opposite of a perfectionist; I could happily tolerate dreadful compromises and asymmetries as long as they worked: Secondly, when faced with despair at ever completing the project, I had been able to hand over the wailing baby to Bill and King.

Bill came up with some remarkable statistics. One in a hundred people in England dream of building their own sailing boat, and of these only one buys the plans to get started. Of those with plans only one in a hundred actually starts building, and of these only one in a hundred actually launch their boat on the water! Finally, of that hardy bunch who get to sail the boat on the sea, only one in a hundred cross the English Channel.

This statistical labyrinth sounded daunting, the chances of sailing this catamaran across the Channel seem disappearingly small. But the gauntlet had been thrown down. **The challenge was to complete the boat and sail it across the Channel,** preferably to Jersey. We would succeed, or go mad in the process. As we learnt more about Polynesian catamarans the goals became more extensive and ideologically sound…

KC
Making money (again)

Money was always needed for the project, and there was never enough of it. One problem was that my brother, Tim, was practically unemployable. Another was that I also, to a lesser extent, was unemployable. Our innate indolence had been sharpened by Miguel (the Spanish waiter from our adolescent days) and any pursuit that we didn't enjoy was abandoned with alacrity. This trait had left me with no money or assets except for an old Morris Minor (what else) and a second hand Aria Pro II electric guitar.

In an attempt to prevent the car being stolen, I tried to emulate Bill by cleverly installing a fuel pump switch behind the glove compartment. It worked fine for a while until one morning, after I flicked on the pump switch and began to drive away, I noticed a bluish smoke filling the car. I turned the engine off, but this didn't help. An alarming smell of burning plastic permeated the air. After gazing moronically at the thickening smoke for a few seconds, I realized what had happened. I released the bonnet catch, leapt out of the car, and pulled the leads off the battery. The wiring to my famous pump switch had shorted to the chassis and converted the loom into a runny mixture of bare wires and molten insulation plastic. Clearly, we would have to keep the boat's electrical system very simple, at least if I was going to have anything to do with it.

One day Tim had a brainwave; why don't we utilize something we like to do, e.g. sailing, with the generation of money? Why don't we teach people to sail? It was brilliant except for one small detail; we didn't know how to teach.
"Teaching's easy! If Bill can do it, so can we." said Tim dismissively. He pointed out that the main obstacle would be a boat, and that we *did* have one of those, the old fireball.
"You want to teach novices how to sail in a Fireball?" I enquired incredulously.
"Why not?"

In fact, when I was about 12, I had already attempted to 'teach' someone how to sail in a Mirror dinghy. I took the parson's son, who had never been in a boat before, out into St. Aubin's bay. After the wind came up we capsized, the first time this had happened to me. The boat then turned turtle, which means the bottom of the boat is now pointing to the sky and the mast is pointing to the bottom of the sea. I was underneath the boat, again a novel experience. My crew was presumably outside because I couldn't see him anywhere. We were always told 'don't let the boat go turtle!' because it's much harder to right it again, so much so that you're as good as doomed. It should have been terrifying, but I suppose because it was so absurd, I was calm. It looked like my time was up and I was peaceful. But what about my crew? I couldn't let him die! Singlehandedly I righted the boat, dragged him on board, bailed the water out and sailed back to shore. He was so frightened he couldn't speak and just sat hunched in the bottom of the boat shivering. His mother was pissed off with me because he had lost one of his shoes. Little did she know that he nearly lost his life.

Tim and I set to work making up a sign on an old wooden surfboard

---

SAILING LESSONS
£4 FOR 1 HOUR

Tim stood by the Fireball in the water whilst I stood with the sign further up the beach, attempting to drum up some custom. The tourists on the beach seemed to just view us as part of the entertainment. They simply sat back and watched me walk up and down like a court jester. Occasionally I would say apologetically,
"Sailing lessons…er, four pounds an hour."
After a while I added,
"Two pounds for half an hour?"
After an interminable time a punter, parts of whom resembled a cooked lobster, finally came along with his son and took up the offer of 2

pounds for 30 minutes. Tim took the son off in the Fireball and I took a break. This couldn't go on. It was too embarrassing.

We put adverts up in local shops and hotels and, after waiting a couple of days, one person rang up. It was another father wanting his son to learn how to sail, which was an excellent intention. This time I met them down at St. Catherine, where the Fireball was kept. The father seemed 'with it' but the son was a vacuous uninterested teenager who looked seriously in need of drifting around the breakwater in a leaky Mirror dinghy. It was clear almost immediately that the boy hadn't exactly volunteered for this and didn't so much as lift a finger to assist me in preparing the boat. I removed the cover, put on the sails, and wheeled 'Spirit' down the slipway, all on my own with the son watching. Then I put the boat in the water, which was unusually and mercifully calm, and took the brat out for an hour. Of course, I had my work cut out just keeping the boat upright and only had the time to occasionally shout out the names of various ropes.

Back on the slipway they watched me take down the sails and then pull the boat back up the slipway, again, all on my own. I was totally knackered. The father then asked the son,

"Well, what did you think of that Andy?"

"Its all right I suppose," Andy replied in a thin weedy voice.

That was the reward for my Herculean efforts. And £4.

Chapter 9

TC

Launch Day

Remarkably, by mid-summer 1987, Bill and I, together with help from King and Patrick, had completed the construction of our Tanenui catamaran. In the Wimborne car park the boat had been entirely assembled, the mast erected and the sails flown. Everything seemed to work, and all that remained was to dissemble her, recommission the trailer, and pull her to the sea.

The plan was simple. My catamaran would be transported in two sections to the Baiter slipway in Poole harbour. There, at low tide, she would be reassembled on the sand and floated by the incoming water. In reality this plan dictated a desperate race against the tide. Small setbacks, that inevitably occur when an ambitious project rests heavily for its success upon the efforts of an unskilled volunteer workforce, mounted up.

As the day wore on, drunkenness and hysterical laughter undermined the efficiency of the operation. Fortunately a lot of people had answered the invitation to the launch party. Harold Bembridge was there (first aid), and a whole van full of the Brighton mob, together with the hardened core of King, Patrick, Susan, Bill and me. Gradually the boat took form. The beams were inserted and bolted home, the netting lashed down, and the decks screwed in place.

Baiter was a rather stony corner of Poole Harbour. A few motor boats bobbed on their moorings in the shallow, muddy water just offshore. Further out in the harbour was our new mooring. This had been professionally laid for us by a large tug equipped with an immense winch. A great concrete disc with chain and swivel was expertly laid, albeit at some expense.

The original plan had been, of course, to lay one ourselves. The wooden Enterprise dinghy was to be loaded up with a Morris Minor engine block (naturally) encased in concrete, and the whole assembly sunk, via a capsize, in the correct place. Thankfully the high likelihood of some grim accident convinced even Bill that, in this rare instance, help was required.

Large, even industrial scale, projects did not usually phase Bill. Immense weights were always susceptible, in his mind, to blocks and tackle. At one stage he had purchased a supposedly "marinised" petrol lorry engine from the local boat auction. "Marinisation" took the form of hideous quantities of oil and grease liberally daubed on all moving and static parts. He bolted this device to a timber staging in the car park. An unlikely extension of galvanised piping functioned as a 15ft angled propeller shaft. A convoluted exhaust appendage completed the contraption. The unit was alarmingly dangerous just to look at. A sort of First World War anti-mine machine. When started up it fulfilled all these expectations, and more.

Great plumes of purple and black smoke blasted from cracks in the exhaust welds, every component vibrated wildly. And this was all in neutral, at low revs. When thrown into gear via the modified Morris gearbox all hell broke loose. The extended propeller shaft whirled around, flailing dangerously. King and I looked on aghast, the noise was incredible. The machine looked like it might break loose from its bonds at any moment and embark on a killing and maiming exercise through Wimborne.

"I'll get it up to full speed!" screamed Bill above the din.

"No, no, no!" we implored. But it was too late; Bill was possessed of one of those savage demonical states. (A similar mechanical passion powered his love of steam engines.) He opened the throttle to full blast; we covered our ears, and watched in horror as the propeller carved great arcs in the smoke. A few moments later the petrol feed pipe tore itself free and, with a couple of backfires, the beast was silenced.

"Remarkable Bill," I said.

You couldn't be too critical at this stage. It would be like telling the mother of an ugly baby the truth. By launch day it had been replaced by a 3 HP 1950's Seagull outboard complete with brass tank and vicious temperament.

Wavelets were lapping around our knees as the final beam bolts were hammered through. Herculean efforts with ropes and blocks saw the masts hauled upright and then, amidst great jubilation, the boat floated! On shore we decided to hold a vote on what her name was to be. The two favourites were "Bunny Cuddles" and "Jumble", and the name Jumble was adopted in a tense final ballot. And so Jumble began, almost immediately, the first of many heroic voyages.

KC
Sailing - at last

Not only did the boat float, but she actually floated to her marks, which suggested that Tim had calculated something correctly at least. Each hull displaced the same amount of water and the fore-and-aft trim was equal. It was quite a triumph. Tim, Bill, Susan and I clambered on board and strutted about the deck whilst the groupies admired from the shore.

"Let's go for a sail! We have the sails on board." Said Tim, full of exuberance.

We hoisted the main and unfurled the Yankee. A breeze filled the sails and we actually moved. Launching Jumble without an immediate sinking was, its true, a prerequisite, but to glide through the water under sail yielded the greatest satisfaction. Even the rudders worked, moving silkily from side to side. Tim looked very happy. We all were, but especially him since this had been a dream for several years now. Susan opened a bottle of cheap champagne and we guzzled it from the very best plastic glasses that Tesco had to offer.

The champagne began to transform the mundane setting of Baiter into a wholly more exotic one. The birth and baptism of a Polynesian catamaran required a tropical ambience and there it was, warm wavelets slapping the sides of the hulls, hot wind through the rigging, natives laughing on the sandy beach, palm tree fronds gently rustling...

Half finished hulls in a garage at the Wimborne car park.

The car park at Wimborne. Note the Peugeot 504 in the foreground and the convertible Morris Minor by the boat.

Cabin tops painted with epoxy paint. Very smart.

KC (standing) and TC (just the head in the background) plus unidentified person (possibly Bill) doing some alignment.

One hull off the Baiter.

Still going.....

At Baiter. One more hull to go.

Both hulls at the launch site. All we have to do now is join them
together.

Launched! KC and TC opening 'champagne'.

Launch day again

TC at helm on our way from Poole to Lyme Regis

KC helming from deckchair. Somewhere south of the Isles of Wight

TC and Patrick preparing dinner, Exmouth.

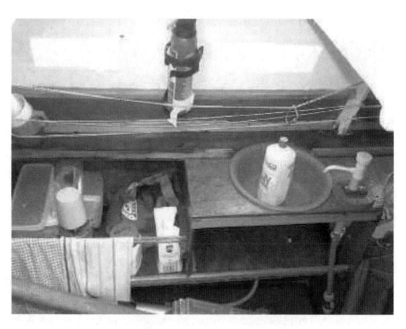

Jumble's kitchen - unusually tidy

Chart table with bunk underneath

Tool room with toolbox

Gorey, Jersey, Channel Islands

Provisions, very old. St Aubin, Jersey.

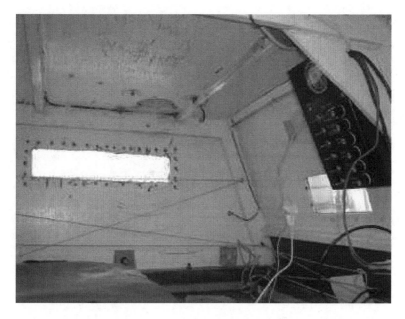

Jumble electronics and view from the inside of the tank windows.

PART 2

Chapter 10

KC

X marks the spot

As soon as the euphoria of the launch died down Tim and I were faced with having to leave Poole and go back home to continue our respective attempts at earning money. The aim was, as is often the case with poor sailors, to get sufficient money to go sailing for a year or maybe longer and then repeat the process. For me the problem with this approach is that you always have, at the back of your mind, the knowing that some sort of dreary work will interrupt the adventure. I just want to go off and not worry about coming back. So Jumble was left in Poole harbour with Bill and Susan.

It was about a month before Tim and I could go back down to the boat. We drove straight to Baiter from Brighton, really quite excited about seeing Jumble again. The idea was to sail around Brownsea Island, (a small island inside Poole harbour which, as a nature reserve with no houses, is very pretty). If the weather held out, we could go off to spend the night in Studland Bay.

It was great to see the boat again, still floating and bobbing happily on the mooring. We quickly got things ready, plugging the fuel line onto the petrol tank, readying the sails and casting off the mooring. We didn't bother with the engine since the wind was blowing in the right direction to get us around and out, and we felt that a boat like Jumble should be purely under sail. I read stories in Sailorman, the Wharram magazine, about Wharram owners who completely eschewed engines and went everywhere, into harbours, up creeks, and into marinas, only using sails. My support for this was to change in the future.

We slipped out of Poole harbour on the gentle breeze and made for Studland Bay, which was about one mile south. Not too ambitious admittedly, but there was no need to rush things. Studland Bay is quite sheltered in everything except a northerly wind and the forecast for the night was a force 2-3 westerly. There should be no problems anchoring there. We wanted a spot close to shore but as far from any other craft as possible. This wasn't difficult as there weren't many boats in the Bay. For her length, 28 feet, Jumble seemed huge, and indeed the deck area was as large as a fifty foot monohull's. There was plenty of room to set up a couple of chairs on opposite sides of a crate for a game of chess.

Despite the shortness of the day's trip I felt very content with things – after all we had actually sailed from A to B on Jumble. This alone is more than the majority of self-build owners achieve. Often, after the launch, the boats will sit on their moorings until they finally become green, cracked and unseaworthy and never get to move under their own sails. The sad fact is that even mass produced boats rarely venture far because their owners have no time to sail them.

After hammering Tim a couple of times at chess, investigating the shoreline in the dinghy, and having dinner at the local pub, it was time for bed. Since there were only 2 of us on board, we had the luxury of a hull each. This was to be our first night afloat. To make that night slightly less worrying we put out another anchor from the stern together with plenty of chain, just in case the wind should change.

I awoke to the sound of a loud bump, as though something was bashing the side of my hull. I shot out of the bunk, and Tim and I arrived, almost naked, simultaneously on deck to see what the hell was going on. Were we aground? Pirates? Then, in dim torchlight, I saw the shape of another yacht worryingly close to Jumble. This was the cause of the bashing sound. The crew, a half-dressed couple, were clambering about the deck with boathooks and oars, trying to fend us off and constantly saying, "sorry", as they should. The wind had indeed shifted to the north during the night and their anchor had dragged. They were battering their way southwards to the shore through an assortment of moored boats, including ours. They slid on by and disappeared into the murky darkness. Amateurs! We checked that our anchors were holding and then went back to bed, sleeping very lightly.

The next day there was no sign of the night visitors. No wreck on the shore. Tim had been studying the local charts.

"King, I think Bill and Susan have been out at sea on Jumble. Look, here's the entry in the log, and there are big crosses on the chart."

He brought the Admiralty chart of the Poole-Isle of Wight area up on deck and spread in out on the slats. There were many large pencil crosses dotted about stretching from Studland to Swanage Bay. Swanage, a pleasant but potentially unsafe anchorage was about another 2 miles south of Studland. Next to the pencil marks, which were virtually engraved into the chart, were times, 12:30, 13:30, 15:10 etc.

"It looks like they went to Swanage," said Tim, perceptively.

"By the look of those fixes, I'd say they were a little unsure of their position. Maybe Bill thinks that the more indelible the cross, the surer the position becomes."

Later Bill confessed that this first trip did turn a bit ugly with the rain arriving unexpectedly. There had been a certain amount of concern on Jumble with the crew occasionally identifying, between increasingly heavy rain showers, the odd headland or steeple for a shaky fix. Swanage as the destination had been abandoned early on and, with a storm approaching, they had fled back to Poole harbour in fear of their very lives.

Desperate Thick Pencil Lines

Susan described to me one of Bill's early battles with the chart in Lyme Bay. Apparently the sea had been choppy and visibility poor, with features on the land seeming to merge and occasionally disappear altogether.

"I think he was a bit nervous since this was the first time he'd had to navigate for real", explained Susan.

Bill had begun to take evermore fixes with the hand-bearing compass, obtaining evermore conflicting results. A bout of obsessive-compulsive disorder seems to have set it. Bill kept shooting below deck to examine the chart, (a manoeuvre in itself not easy for Bill's gangly frame), and then leaping up again like a demented Jack-in-the-box to struggle with another compass fix.

Susan's wave management couldn't have been so good because Jumble shipped a good deal of seawater; the occasional cascade entering the cabin top to soak both Bill and the chart.

"His glasses got so encrusted with salt I'm sure he could see nothing," described Susan,

"He kept mumbling about being unsure of our position, and then started to feel sea-sick".

As waves crashed obliquely against Jumble's bows great plumes of spray would soak Bill and his bobble hat. Still he pressed on with heroic efforts to work out their position. The problem was that he couldn't keep the compass steady enough to obtain a decent fix; it would swing wildly through 45 degrees. Obscured vision and nausea compounded the difficulties.

Finally he had dragged the soaked chart up, flapping wildly in the wind, to show it to Susan at the helm.

"I think we're someone here!" he had shouted. A sweep of his hand indicated the entirety of Lyme Bay - about three hundred square miles. It was clearly of no navigational use. Ever-thicker pencil lines scoured the chart like the hieroglyphics of some ancient aboriginal cave painting. The sun later emerged, the sea calmed and Poole Harbour entrance hoved into view only a couple of miles away. The savagely etched chart remains on Jumble to this day, a symbol of determination of those navigating in heavy weather.

Sailing at sea in a storm is no picnic, and somewhere in the back of Bill's mind there lurked a treacherous, but reasonable, suspicion that Jumble may not be robust enough for anything other than a mild breeze. A proper sea trial was needed to dispel all doubts about Jumble's integrity. Pottering around Poole harbour on a Sunday afternoon, enjoyable as that may be, was not quite what we had in mind for Jumble, and certainly would be unlikely to generate grand stories of nautical bravery and endurance.

Chapter 11

KC
Sea Trials 1988

We were moored up on another yacht's buoy just inside the harbour entrance at Poole. 'We' were Tim, Patrick and myself. We had taken two weeks off work to do this trip in Jumble and for the past two days we had been holed up in her trying to make the best of things. It was blowing a gale and raining just for good measure. We were now sorely tempted just to 'go for it', at least Tim was. He was making noises about the wind seeming to moderate a bit and we could 'probably get to Weymouth in the lull'. The truth of the matter was that the 'lull' resided completely inside Tim's head. Impatience and claustrophobia from being stuck inside the narrow hulls of Jumble had warped his mind. He had forgotten that out there was certain to be a mighty sea that could well spell the end of us. Patrick and I shrank at Tim's insane idea. We preferred to sit in our cramped bunks, stay alive for now, and reflect on the forecast, which had promised a better day tomorrow.

The current weather was certainly a setback, but there had been some successes, or perhaps more accurately triumphs over adversity, up to this point. For instance, Tim and I, in our haste to get the show on the road, had forgotten to tie the tender to the roofrack of Tim's current jalopy. It blew off when we reached 30 mph, smashing a reasonable sized hole in its hull. We took it along anyway, carefully tying it down this time, in the hope that one of us would solve the problem of how to fix it during the twenty minute drive down to Poole harbour. When we met Patrick neither of us had managed to come up with any solutions and just stood there quietly on the shore at Baiter, with our gear waiting expectantly in front of us. There was 100 feet of seawater between us and Jumble. What were we going to do? One thing we were not going to do was go home. We looked around for willing boat-owners-with-tenders but the beach was empty. Then Tim spotted a small circular dinghy along the shore up by the high tide mark. It resembled an Irish coracle in shape and size, about 4 feet in diameter, and looked like it would be very unstable. Although I took the moral high ground saying that it was wrong to take without asking and that you 'wouldn't like it if someone did it to you', Tim and Patrick were sure the owner wouldn't miss it for a few days, if indeed the coracle even had an owner considering its shabby condition. We were only borrowing it, they told me, and so it got us, precariously, to Jumble. After a while our new tender looked at home strapped down on the port bow.

On day three we broke out of Poole and began our odyssey. The wind had moderated to a force 5 but the sea was still a bit rough and we began to get wet almost immediately. All this was acceptable but there was another problem; the wind was southwesterly which meant beating to windward in a boat that doesn't beat. You cannot afford to point too close to the wind otherwise she will just stop moving and drift sideways due to the large amount of windage. Worse still is going into 'irons', (pointing directly into the wind and going nowhere). On Jumble it was very hard to break out and get moving again. So we had to sail well off the wind and keep boat speed up. Quite often we would come to a complete stop when the helmsman had failed to efficiently negotiate the series of waves up ahead.

To get to Exmouth you have to sail around Portland Bill, a large headland west of Weymouth, and the trick is to avoid the two sets of overfalls off the Bill by sailing between them. The alternative was to sail way offshore, adding many more miles and hours to our journey. I favoured going all the way out to sea and around that way since it was the least scary option, and I persuaded the others that this was best. After three hours of hard grind, a fix was taken, quickly to avoid vomiting on the chart table, and it was discovered that we had only gone 10 miles. Tim broke the news to us.

"If we go the sea route we may not make it back in 'til dark. I don't fancy that. I vote we tuck in between the overfalls. It will cut at least 3 hours off. Also, we haven't got a chance of making Exmouth and at this rate we'll be lucky to get as far as Lyme Regis."

I went down to look at the chart myself. From our last fix we were about 30 miles from Lyme Regis as the crow flies. This fix put us 3 miles south of Portland Bill. Exmouth was about 50 miles away and dead into wind. I had to admit that Tim was right and we should make for Lyme Regis. I too was not enamoured with the idea of a night landfall. The gap between the overfalls it would have to be, and I studied details of the Bill. It wasn't pretty. The squiggly parallel lines indicating overfalls were definitely there, a mile off the Bill and there again 2 miles off, so we had a gap of a mile to shoot for. Big enough, one would think. On the chart next to the squiggly lines it said 'heavy overfalls'. Lovely. I emerged grim-faced from the chartroom. Patrick and Tim both had their hoods up as it was now raining and they too looked a little anxious.

"How far are we from the gap King," shouted Patrick from the helm.

"About 4 miles. We could probably tack now." I said. This we did with some difficulty but eventually with the yankee and staysail fully backed and plenty of swishing on the tillers we slewed round onto port tack. Our bearing was now 330 degrees, taking us in the general direction of the gap. After about half an hour we could make out the white of the overfalls but it was white everywhere and the 'gap' was worryingly absent.

"All I can see is overfalls. Where is your gap Tim?" said Patrick, anxiously.

"Just a bit nearer Patrick. Don't worry. There! Look! I think I can see it," said Tim pointing into the white ahead. I saw nothing but foam and knew now that there was no 'gap' and that Tim had been lying to us. In five minutes we were in them, the worst of the overfalls, being bashed around from side to side and holding on for grim death. It was as though we were in breakers. I thought I could see Patrick praying. On several occasions the boat stopped dead in the water after hitting the front of a wave and if the tide hadn't been in our favour, we would have simply gone backwards. Finally the white turned to green again and we had entered Lyme Bay, for which I was truly grateful.

"What happened to the gap?" said Patrick, shaken.

"I don't know. I suspect we were much closer to the Bill than we thought and were in fact in the middle of the inner overfalls. It was a bit nasty." said Tim.

Three hours later we were within a few hundred metres of the small Cobb entrance. The tide was ebbing and the engine was at full speed for fear that we wouldn't get into the harbour before it emptied. We got through the entrance but then hit the bottom and were stuck, blocking the harbour. On the pier I could see a couple of old fishermen shaking their heads sadly at our incompetence.

Later that day, Tim, Patrick and I were sitting on the sand in the corner of Lyme Regis harbour. It was evening, August, still warm. Patrick had just lit our driftwood fire, which immediately became quite a blaze. Tim had given it a good chance of igniting with some petrol. He had always liked fire and I'm quite surprised that he wasn't one of those foolish teenagers who blew his fingers off making homemade fireworks. He did, however, make his mark in our neighbourhood when only 8 years old. We lived in Sycamore Avenue, a middle class area, which was next to Kevin Close, a lower class area. Of course as little boys we weren't aware of the distinction, but we did know that one just didn't venture into Palace Close. With an armed escort maybe it was possible, but under normal circumstances it was practically suicide. Apart from the general feeling of dread that Kevin Close instilled in us, there was the fact that the deeply sinister and just plain demonic superbully Paul Arnold lived there. It was the fact that you might meet *him* that kept us away. I imagined that he could do terrible things just by his evil radiation. So we Sycamore Avenue boys didn't venture down there.

One day, however, I saw a fire engine go past our house and down the road to Kevin Close. Something was up. A little later that evening there was a knock on the door. It was a policeman. Tim's version of events was that he and Gary Bunion and another boy were attempting to make a small fire using what they thought were abandoned tomato crosses. Of course the fire quickly got out of hand and they were unable to put it out. It jumped from their small pile of crosses to a bigger pile a few feet away and then to Kevin Close's small forest, causing quite a conflagration with trees and all going up in flames. Terrified by the turn of events they ran away. The others escaped but Tim was cornered by none other than Paul Arnold. Arnold, though, was apparently deeply impressed by the sheer magnitude of the fire and therefore didn't beat my brother to a pulp on the spot. He simply said

"You're in big trouble now". Which was true.

Also, there were lots of worried adults around, worried that their houses were about to be burned down, so I suppose Arnold had to hold back.

Despite this early experience, Tim still liked fire.

I had just finished gutting the mackerel we had caught that afternoon, for dinner. Tim had found an old piece of iron grating on the beach which we used to rest the fish on as they cooked in tin foil. Patrick cracked open some wine, literally, with a winch handle since Jumble's one and only corkscrew had disappeared. He just smashed the top off the bottle with one swift stroke. I felt particularly content with the world after our exploits of the day, a hard beat from Weymouth, surviving the overfalls, an awkward entry into the Cobb, Lyme Regis' tiny harbour, and now a mug of cheap red wine in one hand.

"I really enjoyed that sail today. How about you Patrick?" I said. Patrick was the newest quarter-owner of Jumble and Tim and I hoped he would be happy with his recent investment.

"Yes, fantastic. I have to say Jumble is a bit wet though. The water just comes up in sheets through the deck slats. In a monohull's cockpit area you wouldn't get wet like that." Patrick was a bit of a conservative when it came to boat design and seaworthiness and indeed just general comfort around a yacht. We had to bring the positive points of cat sailing to his attention. Tim began the task,

"True. But the boat's designed that way. The idea is that when a particular combination of strong wind and large wave finally arrives one day, the boat won't capsize because the water will actually flow through the deck, dissipating the turning force. It would be very hard to capsize this catamaran Patrick." Patrick thought about it and, after another swig of wine said,

"But if you did capsize, that would be it! Not so easy to right again. Unlike a monohull which tends to right itself. After all, it has that heavy keel as counterweight." Tim continued,

"It's precisely that heavy keel that will take you like a stone to the bottom. Most monohulls have no extra buoyancy and as soon as the cabin fills with water down it goes. A cat, especially a wooden one like Jumble, can't sink."

The fish was done, perhaps even a little overdone judging by the mushiness of the flesh. We picked at it with our fingers, eating carefully and trying to avoid swallowing any of the many bones mackerel possess. As a matter of fact, the two miserable puny fish we were sharing did not really have the makings of a hearty supper, tasty though they were, and I went back to the boat to try and find something else edible. Half a loaf of stale french bread and a tin of sardines was all I could come up with. Tim looked disappointed and, despite our financial shortcomings, felt action was needed.

"Let's go out for dinner tomorrow."

It's about 60 miles from Lyme Regis to Plymouth across Lyme bay and it was going to be a tall order to make it in one day. The weather, as it had been all week, was not great; cloudy, force 4 westerly with the constant threat of rain. It was decided to make for Exmouth instead and we slogged across the bay, beating through the nasty waves until we could finally tack onto a course for the mouth of the Ex.

We could finally see the entrance to the river. The almanac told us that it was a very narrow entrance and in fact each of us *thought* we could make out the river mouth, but in reality we had picked on some other coastal detail. The grey mass of Exmouth was becoming clearer and clearer until indeed, there was the mouth. The plan was simple enough; enter the river Ex and find a suitable mooring, tie up, then go ashore for a splendid meal. When we got within half a mile we went through the arrival routine: Lowering the Johnson into the water and attempting to start it, as well as concentrating very hard on everything and becoming anxious. It turned out that the tide was with us going in which contributed to a polished entry for the watching gallery, although I was a bit alarmed at just how much the tide was in our favour, perhaps 3 or 4 knots. We lowered the sails and had the Johnson just ticking over but we were still belting up-river. Tim was the first to lose his composure.

"Grab onto that buoy over there! I'll try to get it on the port bow."

The buoy in question was another yacht's mid-channel mooring buoy, without the yacht. Patrick and I positioned ourselves on each bow of Jumble, in case Tim screwed it up, and waited. Of course the buoy went between the hulls whereupon Patrick and I dashed over to the anchor opening and grabbed the slippery ball, holding on for dear life. The force of the tide pulling the boat was immense and it was all we could do to keep hold. Tim's attempts to put the outboard into reverse failed but finally I got a loop of rope around the base of the buoy and cleated it off. We had arrived.

As luck would have it our temporary mooring was only about 10 metres from the yacht club, right opposite us. I was very hungry and could already taste the food in my mouth, fish and chips, peas, bread and butter, as we untied the coracle and plopped it into the water. Within a few minutes we would be in the club restaurant gorging ourselves. Carefully the three of us got into the tender and adjusted our positions so as to reduce the chance of a capsize. Then, with Tim and I wielding the paddles, off we forged to the riverbank and jetty. What we hadn't taken into account was the current that had delivered us here so swiftly in the first place. As soon as Patrick let go of Jumble the tide took us at a considerable lick upriver. It was one foot across and 10 feet down. Within 30 seconds we had travelled quite a long way at right angles to where we wanted to go, the yacht club already distant and receding agonizingly further by the second. We finally reached the riverbank about half a mile upstream, getting rather wet in the process due to the flailing of paddles and the necessity to wade ashore prematurely. Half an hour later we arrived at the club, exhausted, wet, and very very hungry.

Two weeks is not enough time to go sailing comfortably. It seemed that we had hardly arrived in Exmouth, when the week was already up and we had to think about going back again. Even more irritating was the fact that the first two days were spent in harbour as a result of the weather, a factor which was always threatening to scupper the whole venture at any time. The forecast was not good; storms were due from the southwest within the next 24 hours, if not sooner. We had to make a decision to either stay in Exmouth and possibly have to leave the boat there, returning for her another time, or to go while it was still only a force 4. It's a long way to Exmouth by car or train, and Tim, who was completely intolerant of journeys by either mode of transport any longer than 5 minutes duration, was keen to get going. There were other problems with leaving the boat; where could Jumble be moored for at least a few weeks, and what would be the cost of whatever mooring we might find? Patrick and I agreed we should go, although I could picture large black cumulonimbus formations eagerly speeding their way to us. The sooner we went, the better.

We motored out into the channel and raised the sails. As soon as we left the shelter of land the sea became quite rough and wind whistled through the rigging. The sky was overcast and a cold, green colour. All a bit daunting. This time, however, the wind was behind us and the 45 miles to Weymouth would only take about 5 hours. Also, the sea always looks less intimidating when you are running, with the wind behind you.

We were flying along at more than 8 knots and the motion, the Wharram 'bob', was fine – you get to learn how to anticipate each wave and move with it. The motion of a catamaran is very different to a monohull; cats generally don't pitch and roll but sort of bobble about from corner to corner with a much smaller amplitude.

After an hour or so I saw Tim glancing behind us more and more frequently. There they were, about 12 hours in advance of the forecast. Large, almost black storm clouds, catching us rapidly.

"King, Patrick. We won't get round Portland Bill before they reach us. I think we should go into Lyme Regis."

I was very happy to agree to this. The wind was picking up and we put a reef in the main. The vanguard of the maelstrom, low grey scudding clouds, was already with us and I could feel little spits of rain on my face and hands. The whole sky was becoming prematurely darker and it had the look and feel of a Turner seascape, complete with a small shaft of sunlight briefly peeking through between the huge black clouds.

Even though we could clearly see the Cobb, it was still about 30 minutes away and I was concerned we wouldn't get there before the gale arrived. We could see lightening and heavy downpours emanating from the beast just behind us and we had to put another reef in the main. When we slipped into the Cobb, the tide was mercifully high, and we tied ourselves to a vacant mooring buoy with that familiar feeling of relief.

Chapter 12

TC

Lyme Regis to Weymouth. Night Passage from Hell.

King had returned to accountancy slavery in Jersey. Patrick and I were left onboard Jumble in Lyme Regis harbour. We huddled below decks and listened to the BBC deliver the weather forecast.

In fact, huddling below was a bit of a performance since accommodation was spartan and, to be frank, required a reasonable degree of dexterity, subtlety of mind and limb and – let's face it – gymnastic ability. To get into a bunk, for instance, required hanging onto the sides of the cabin whilst sliding one's legs underneath the chart table and beam support stringer. There was no room to sit upright. Once in, getting out was a major operation that involved slithering forward, snake-like, until one was in a position to grasp upwards. In wet weather, two people could sit facing one another across the twin steps down into the cabin. Adjectives such as 'roomy' or 'spacious' clearly didn't apply, whilst 'bijou' and 'compact' did. Occasionally, 'claustrophobic', 'impossibly small', 'absurdly tiny' were bantered around in cheerful, perhaps hysterical, parlance.

The news was not as we wished; the light westerlies of the night were going to give way to rain and strong winds within 48 hours. We stared at the chart by the light of the paraffin lamp.

"I think we might have to make a night passage," I said.

Patrick's eyes darkened, he didn't like night passages.

"If we leave in, say, two hours we should have a favourable tide to take us round Portland Bill," I continued.

Patrick couldn't escape the devastating logic. Either we sailed overnight or we risked being holed up in Lyme Regis for the foreseeable future. We ate up our pasta and sardines with baked beans in an atmosphere of grim resolution.

The prospect of a night passage would have been more acceptable if it were not for the giant obstacle of Portland Bill. This great hook of land forces the tidal flow of the Channel to surge and cascade in the most frightening of manners. If a strong wind was blowing against the run of the tide the conditions could sink a small yacht. We had come this way already, in good conditions, and it had been rough.

Moreover, since the wind was light, we both knew we would have to attempt the inner passage. This would involve sailing close to the shore in the pitch dark. Patrick, as I knew, nurtured an especial fear of rocks at night, a fear that bordered on the irrational.

But the die was cast and by nine o'clock we were sailing away from Lyme Regis with all sails up. At first spirits were high and Jumble jogged along at a healthy 5 knots, but by 11 p.m. as we approached the Bill, the wind began to drop. Patrick attempted to start the Evinrude, but the engine knew something was up and resolutely refused to start. I had a crack at the Beast, but to no avail. We resorted to the Johnson. Patrick eyed up the engine as a well known respected foe. He swept in and smartly pulled the starting rope, this promptly snapped and sent him reeling back across the deck. The Johnson remained silent. Two engines were down and we had one left, the Seagull.

By now the wind had fallen to calm and we were simply being swept along by the considerable tide. There was an eerie swell, but the surface of the sea itself was oily smooth, and in the distance we could hear the tolling bell of the "Outer Owers". This bell was mounted on a huge steel navigation buoy moored off the Bill. It was the size of a small ship.

Still we drifted, unable to steer, in about 6 knots of tide. The bell donged, ever nearer, a great clamour in the night. Then, silhouetted against dim horizon, I saw the buoy itself, terrifyingly close and on a direct collision course.

Patrick saw it too, and stared at it open-mouthed. The bell donged a great reverberating dong of doom and Patrick began making strange noises like a reprimanded Stan Laurel. At this speed we could easily smash open a hull on impact. I seized hold of the Seagull starter pull chord, opened the fuel line, adjusted the choke and hauled for all I was worth.

With a great bang and clouds of smoke the unloved Seagull exploded into life. It was a miracle. Jumble gathered steerage way through the water, and with metres to spare we avoided the buoy. The Seagull kept going in its inimitable suicidal fashion, and we awarded it an immediate George Cross as we proceeded towards Weymouth.

By the following evening we had arrived back on our mooring at Baiter. The coracle was returned, with its real owner catching us at it which was very embarrassing. In our defense I said,
"Sorry. We thought it had been abandoned."
But of course on reflection I could see that this was actually an insult to the owner.

Soon the hardships and terrors of the voyage were forgotten. They were, indeed, transmogrified into gloriously heroic episodes – fondly recalled over cups of tea by safe firesides.

The next morning a man who had been staring at Jumble for a while from the shore at Baiter came up to me.
"Excuse me," he said, "Did you ever watch that film where the four-engine propeller driven plane crash lands in the desert?"
"Yes..." I had a feeling I knew where this was leading.
"You know, the one where the crazy German model aeroplane designer convinces them to rebuild it, only as a monoplane with the survivors all strapped to the wings?"
"Yes..."
"Only he doesn't tell them he's a model aircraft engineer until they're about to try and take off for the nearest oasis?"
"Yes...it was called 'The Flight of the Phoenix'."
"Yes! That was it! Well, your boat reminds me of that! A large well-found vessel that has been ravaged on some desert island and the survivors have been inspired by some lunatic to construct a life-raft with a mast from the remainder!"
"Thank you." I replied somewhat sardonically.

Jumble generated a wide range of responses but a disconcertingly large number were orientated around this bizarre life-raft theme. I think it was partly due to the fact that she was so low slung in the water, and the windows were on the small side, and the beams holding the hulls together were evidently planks of 'two by four's' glued unceremoniously together.

Chapter 13

KC
Sid

Despite all our attempts at frugality, the cost of running a boat was beginning to cause a strain. The expenses, even for a raft, were still considerable and the upcoming winter mooring fee of £300 was due to be paid. Tim was always on the lookout for potential part-owners and one day he casually told me he thought he had found us another partner. This person was the friend of an acquaintance who was looking for just this sort of opportunity. His name was Sid. I tried to find out a little more information from Tim,

"Who is this bloke?"

"He's a friend of Nick. Apparently they go way back."

"What does he do?" I asked.

"I'm not sure. Something to do with computers? He seems really keen. I think we should go for it – we really need the cash."

I wasn't so sure. Everybody involved with Jumble up to this point had been friends of Tim, but this person was a complete stranger.

"What if we don't like him? At least one of us should meet him." Tim, though, had already decided that Sid was going to be a fine chap and for him it was just a matter of how soon he could put the money in the bank.

"Ah, he'll be OK. Look, he probably won't even want to do any sailing. It's probably just the idea of being able to say he owns part of a yacht. I'm going to phone him tonight. If it really doesn't work out, we can always buy him out."

I thought that was going to be unlikely since we would have to find the money to buy him out. Also, what if he didn't want to sell back his share?

"King, I wouldn't worry about it."

So I didn't. We met Sid a couple of weeks later, after he had become a fully paid up partner of the Jumble syndicate, at a pub in Brighton. He was about 5'9", around fifty years old, and wore John Lennon glasses.

"Sid, this is my brother King." Sid shook my hand feebly and smiled, exposing an ugly mouthful of poorly maintained teeth.

"Hello. That's a funny name. King. Never heard that before". Sid said, with an inane expression on his long curved face. I realised then that he looked a bit like the man-in-the-moon.

"It's short for Kingsley, Sid." I explained, somewhat irritated. "How much sailing have you done?" I asked, cutting out the customary small talk. He didn't answer me straight away and instead spent an extended period of time finishing his pint, which was not his first.

"Oh, this and that." said Sid, evasively. Eventually he disclosed that he had owned a boat a few years ago although upon questioning, it appeared that he didn't seem to remember much about it. Sid's charisma was vanishingly small and I didn't foresee enjoying too many hearty laughs with him on the deck of Jumble, or anywhere. This was Tim's idea and he could test out the sailing first with our new friend.

Somehow, however, due to clever manoeuvring on Tim's part, I ended up at Shoreham yacht club getting Jumble ready to go sailing with my new best mate Sid. Much to my annoyance, he actually turned up, and on time. For the past few weeks he had been pestering us to go sailing and when he threatened to take Jumble out on his own, he forced my hand.

"Hello King!" hailed Sid cheerfully. He had that silly grin on his face again.

"Hello Sid," I replied, trying not to sound too unenthusiastic.

"I've already been on board this morning, checking a few things."

Checking what exactly Sid? He was already irritating me. What was he doing on my boat without me? But of course, now he owned part of Jumble too and was perfectly entitled to go on board whenever he wished. This was an unpleasant truth. It just didn't seem right.

"What were you checking?" I asked suspiciously.

"To make sure the charts of the Channel were on board, and that the paint had dried."

"What paint? What were you painting?" The idea of him permanently putting his mark on Jumble was almost too much.

"Oh, a bit of the deck."

"Hmm. Charts of the Channel? We're only going for a sail to Brighton pier and back."

"I know, but it's best to be prepared, King."

Despite Jumble's usual egalitarian command structure, I felt that today I had to establish my authority otherwise there may be serious consequences involving my hands and his scrawny neck.

"All right Sid. Can you untie the mainsail? I'll sort out the engine."

As I fiddled with the Evinrude I considered whether or not I was being a bit unfair in my assessment of the man. Possibly, but something told me he was a complete nincumpoop and that today would be an exercise in damage limitation. I got the engine going and we cast off. I assumed control of the helm and engine and Sid's job was to fend off the other boats, if necessary, as we left. We were moving out into the channel with no problems when I heard a shout,

"Watch out! You're going to hit that big pole over there!"

"Sid. Don't worry. We are in no danger of hitting the pole."

He was looking genuinely concerned and appeared to be breathing heavily. I thought of abandoning the whole venture right then, but inertia carried me forward. Instead, to calm him down, I tried talking to him.

"So Sid, what do you do? I mean, to keep the wolf from the door."

"Computers. I work in computers."

"Oh? Are you a programmer?"

Sid looked at me quizzically.

"You know, coding." I said. Sid was still looking at me puzzled but then suddenly seemed to remember.

"Yes, yes, I do a bit of that. And other things. Actually I've only recently moved into computers. I was in sales for many years. Washing machines."

That's more like it. We were nearly at the river mouth and I asked Sid to raise the main and unfurl the yankee, which he did. Soon we were sailing and I cut the engine. As soon as the infernal outboard noise is gone and all you can hear is wind, waves and seagulls, everything is suddenly much more enjoyable. I even felt kindly disposed towards Sid and we chatted about life. He told me he had a daughter and that he had spent some time in the USA and Mexico. I was surprised at this adventurous behaviour, and almost impressed. As we were talking I felt the boat drag a little and then we stopped going through the water altogether. I quickly inspected the sea around the hulls. We had caught a fishing buoy which was now snarled up between the port rudder and the hull. Sid looked alarmed.

"What is it? What happened?"

"We're stuck on a fishing buoy. We need to depower the boat. Can you free off the yankee and staysail?"

Because of the tide, Jumble was straining like a dog on a leash and all the time the rope caught behind the rudder was getting wedged tighter and tighter. Sid seemed to be paralysed on the foredeck. All he had to do was to undo a couple of ropes.

"Sid! What's the matter? We need to release the sheets."

Still he didn't move, his eyes looking wild and scared. I went forward to let them go myself when he leapt up.

"I can do it! I'll do it!"

I left him and went to get the oar to try freeing the fishing buoy by pushing down on the rope. Then I heard a loud thrashing noise. I turned around to see the Yankee attempting to rip itself to shreds. Sid had only managed to half release the sheet, which was now in a mess of knots on the winch.

"Sid, pull in the roller reefing line!" I had to shout above the noise of the thrashing sail. He looked at me as though I were speaking in a strange tongue, and then darted below decks. I assumed he had simply abandoned me and I went back to freeing the rope. I had nearly succeeded when he startled me by reemerging, grasping the kitchen knife.

"I have to cut the sheets! It's the only way!" said Sid. Clearly this small crisis had driven him half-crazy.

"Don't cut the sheets!" I said, trying to adopt the tone of a sergeant-major. "Pull that red rope over there and cleat it off!"

I gave one more push down on the oar and the rope came free, slipping under the rudder and shooting off downside. Sid hadn't moved. With the boat now sailing again the yankee began to fill and the terrible thrashing largely stopped.

"Sid, put the knife away." I said in measured tones, as though I were talking to a homicidal maniac. Slowly he came round and the glaze from his eyes lifted. As he returned the weapon to the galley I could hear him mutter

"We were in big trouble there. Big trouble."

I gybed Jumble and went straight back to the marina.

I found out later from Tim that Sid's time in Mexico was largely spent in a Mexican jail, allegedly as a result of illegal dealings in certain sorts of plant life. This was a startling revelation, not so much that he was an ex-con, but that he had survived prison. I told Tim that we absolutely had to get rid of Sid on the grounds that he was a complete and utter fool and may well kill us all at sea.

Chapter 14

KC
Keyhaven to Poole 1988-89

I had traveled down from London to Keyhaven, which is 40 miles east of Poole, with all my sailing stuff, to meet Bill. In fact I first went to his house and we discussed our planned voyage which was to be from Keyhaven to Poole. There wasn't much to plan since it was a simple hop across Poole Bay and we would be in sight of land all the way. Our only problem was to make sure that we negotiated the Shingles bank. Keyhaven is tucked away between Christchurch and Lymington, opposite Yarmouth on the Isle of Wight. With a cursory look at the chart it is easy to think that you can just pop out of the river Key and then turn west for Poole. On closer inspection, however, you notice a long string of what looks like pebbles stretching southwest all the way from the mouth of the river, almost to the Needles. By the pebbles is written 'dries' etc. I hate it when the chart says things like that. What it means is that the Shingles bank is very dangerous and you should stay clear of it. Therefore it meant that we had to sail all the way to its outer limit before turning west.

I put my bags in Bill's old car and off we went to Jumble. He and Susan had sailed the boat from Poole to Keyhaven a few weeks previously and I was keen to see where she was lying. Bill mentioned to me something about "inlet of the river" and "mud" but I had convinced myself that accessing the boat would mean just a few paces across the sand, or at worst a short journey in the inflatable. The reality was a little different. Bill pulled up about half a mile from the boat, which really was in an inlet of the river. It was one of many craft that were arranged snake-like along the inlet. We had timed it to be there at high tide so as minimise the mud crossing, and indeed there was Jumble, floating happily.

Bill and I got the dinghy out and began to inflate it with the foot pump. The rubber folds seemed to take an age to uncurl and it took us fully 20 minutes. To be honest we were both a little tired at the end of it.

We carried it down to the water and then loaded up with our bags, food etc. It was decided that Bill would row since he understood the mechanics of oars and rowlocks a bit better than I. My job was to stop anything falling out and to keep my bum dry. Off we went. Jumble was only about 200 feet away and it was going to be one of the quickest tender journeys on record. Half way there the water started to drain away and, to my horror, in a couple of minutes Jumble was sitting on the mud. It was as though a giant had pulled the plug out. I pointed out the sinister turn of events to Bill and he said "Yes, the tide goes out quickly here, I don't think we're going to make it".

Bill, I thought, we already haven't made it. Soon we too were aground. The sea had gone and all that remained was mud, reeds, and marooned boats in the channel. I knew what he was thinking; maybe this will be the good type of mud that is only a few centimetres thick. We both had Wellington boots on which was fortunate, or not, depending on the type of mud. You see, there can also be the 'bad' type of river inlet mud which may be feet thick. We got out of the dinghy and plopped our boots into the sludgy stuff. It felt 'good' – maybe this wouldn't be a nightmare after all. Jumble was a mere 50 feet away and we walked gingerly along hoping that the mud would remain 'good', pulling the tender alongside trying to skim it over the remaining shallow pools of seawater that were left. About 20 feet from the boat the mud turned 'bad' and our progress slowed abruptly. Our boots were sinking ever deeper with each step into the black stuff; 1 inch, 2 inches, 4 inches, maybe a six incher. We held onto one another for support as we attempted to extract our boots. They came out with a deep squelching sound. Then it was 8 inches of mud, which is a lot. Too much in fact to walk through in boots, so off they came and were thrown into the tender, immediately making everything filthy.

We carried on, maybe only 10 feet from Jumble now, in bare feet and rolled up trousers. The mud would ooze up between my toes and then slide up my ankle enveloping my calf. The trick was to keep the momentum going and get the other foot down before it went past the knee. Then we started falling over rendering futile all our attempts to keep the stinking stuff off our clothes. I took off my shirt and threw it in the dinghy which, incidentally, was becoming a burden to pull, despite its slipperiness. Bill and I were now a sorry sight, crawling through the mud inch by inch, completely covered in the stuff. Finally we got to the boat and hauled ourselves into the front netting. We had very little water on board, and that was for drinking, so all the clothes and boots were left in the tender until later when the sea came back. What a nightmare. We chose a hull each and then decided a bottle of wine would be an appropriate reward for our ordeal. Tomorrow, Poole.

The Evinrude started at the 20th pull and I began to raise the anchor. Bill tended carefully to the choke, which needed to be adjusted in a precise manner or the engine would stop. Off we went, down the muddy channel and out into the Solent. I went below into the chartroom, which overlapped my bunk by about a foot, and studied the chart. I scrutinised the Shingles Bank again. It was over to our starboard side under a few feet of water. It was actually quite lumpy out in the channel and I thought I could see the Bank, a long spit of white water. Small overfalls, my favourite.

We raised the sails; the main, jib and yankee, and laid a course for the Needles, about 180 degrees. As soon as we were in the Solent proper we felt the full strength of the force 4-5 westerly and got wet within a few minutes. We were on a reach, easy sailing, but there was wind against tide which meant the sea was a bit rough. On we went past the Shingles Bank until we both agreed it would be safe to turn west towards Poole, and so we hardened up to about 220 degrees. We were in for a long slog beating all the way. The good thing about this trip was that we were always in sight of land, so we knew where we were. It was possible to navigate by just looking around, the sort of navigating I relish.

As we approached Poole about 6 hours later Bill and I began to do some preliminary worrying about the chain ferry that runs across the 50 metre entrance to the harbour. It trundles back and forth, at about 10 miles an hour, all day long and is unstoppable. This means that if you time it wrong then you get hit. With the current wind direction and strength I thought we could sail elegantly and effortlessly through the gap and impress the onlookers. Bill was less sure and began to lower the outboard.

"Better safe than sorry King."

"Yes, you're right. We should keep it ticking over just in case."

After quite a bit of effort he got the engine going and throttled it back to idle. The ferry had just crossed over in front of us and was unloading its cargo of vehicles and people. "That should take some time" I thought. It was about 6 p.m. and the wind was easing off but still we were moving along quite nicely, 50 feet or so from the entrance. Then I heard the clank-clank of the chain and the ferry began to move again. As we got closer to the opening it was becoming clear that at our existing speed we would be uncomfortably close to the ferry which was inexorably advancing at right angles in front of us. Bill obviously felt the same way, put the Evinrude into gear and gave it some welly, doubling our speed. Then, in mid-entrance, the engine stopped. We could see the crew of the ferry and indeed now could hear them shouting at us to get out of the way. This was desperate and very embarrassing.

"Bill we have to get the engine started."

"I know!"

He pulled on the starter rope like a madman to no avail. I took over, first adjusting the choke, the only variable I had any confidence to change. Abandoning the helm, Bill feverishly squeezed the fuel nipple as I pulled and pulled. Lots of shouting from the ferry now, which was unhelpful. Finally the beast got going again and we eased out of their way. I heard things like "fools" "shouldn't be on the water" "incompetent" plus some general abuse in our direction.

Tim put the phone down and turned to face me, his face ashen.

"What is it?" I said.

"It's Patrick. He's pulling out of Jumble." It was a bit of a bombshell, especially coming on the heels of the Sid debacle.

"Why? Why is he doing that?"

"He and Bill didn't see eye-to-eye."

That was it then. We should have taken more precautions to avoid the two of them getting to know each other too well. In hindsight it was obvious they would lock horns. Patrick hadn't given Tim all the gory details, but it appeared that the catalyst for the fallout was the engine that Bill had obtained three months previously. Patrick said to Bill, probably a bit too bluntly, that the monster petrol engine was totally wrong for Jumble. In this Patrick was completely correct. Bill, his pet project under attack, took umbrage and they had a flaming argument. Patrick's departure was a serious blow. Apart from the fact that he was a good sailor and fun in general to have on board, we now had to find £1,000 to buy him out.

Chapter 15

KC
Accounting

In one of the greatest sacrifices of the modern age, I began a real job in an accountancy firm. Tim desperately tried to talk me out of it, but the money had to come from somewhere, and I was led to believe, or perhaps convinced myself, that I would be a millionaire in three years and that, despite Monty Python, it wouldn't be so bad.

The first shock was the fact that I had to 'work' until 5:30 p.m., when I had thought it was 5:00 p.m. I was incredulous and argued my case vehemently until it was pointed out in the contract. Another setback was attire; after day three I was taken aside by one of the assistant managers and asked if I knew what a suit was. What I had assumed to be acceptable dress, an eclectic mix of old trousers, shirts and jackets, was deemed to be inappropriate. So I went in search of, and bought, the cheapest suit in the whole of the island, bar none. I looked a complete idiot in it. A tie was also part of the rules so I had to get one of those too. I looked a complete idiot in that as well. Then there was the work itself. Accountancy firms make their money by doing audits for other businesses. This means that they look over the financial book-keeping of the other company and, after relieving them of a bunch of money, say that the books are OK, that this company really did make 'said amount' of money and that they really do have the stated assets.

I was sent out as a gofer with some 'qualified' member of staff from the office to personally visit the client company. The first thing you realize is that the client, despite evidence to the contrary, hates you. In fact it's not so much the client, but their accounting department employees that hate you. After all, you are coming in to see if they are doing their job properly. We took along something called the 'working papers' which was a copy of the work done for the previous year's audit, and we used this to assist us. The trick was to copy those working papers, changing the odd number here and there, and of course the date. My partner would make a big show of getting large reams of papers out of his briefcase and arrange them around the copy of the 'working papers'. I would be sent off to retrieve bank statements and other such fascinating documents.

Another safe task for me was to add up a large quantity of numbers to see if they amounted to the expected total. I never came up with the right total, and would state confidently that the 'right' figure was actually wrong. My anal partner would add it up, make no mistakes, and come up with the correct number. As this was often repeated at different venues I began to get the feeling that this wasn't the game for me.

When I was in the office, which became more and more frequent, the tedium had the effect of making time virtually stand still. In one sense this was good because life appeared to last longer, but the cruel catch was that I couldn't do anything interesting in that extra time. What I did do was arrange the investment accounts of someone's retirement portfolio. All the bits and pieces pertaining to the portfolio were contained in a cardboard box, and each morning for several weeks it sat by my desk waiting for me to arrive each day. I would take all the papers out and arrange them on the desk in various piles. Somehow I had to extract numbers from these piles and put them onto paper in a meaningful way, but I didn't have a clue what I was doing, even with access to the previous year's accounts. Since this was considered the simplest task that could be asked of me I naturally couldn't ask anyone for help, and when someone enquired as to the status of the project I replied that it was all going swimmingly. Eventually, after a month had passed and the whole thing still incomplete, I discovered, one morning, that my box was missing. Later the same day I was summoned to the office of Linus Owen, the manager responsible for the job. My box was on the floor beside him.

"Kingsley, Monmouth Investments still isn't finished."

"No, not quite. But I'm nearly there."

He looked through my papers and numbers and after a while said,

"Parts A and D, interest receivable and stock movement, are outstanding."

"Linus, you know, I thought they were pretty damn good myself." Linus looked at me, puzzled.

"I don't mean they were any good. I meant that they are not there."

I was a serf, Linus was a serf, we were all serfs to the partners. It was no better than the Dark Ages. I soon realized that the big bucks only came after years of junior servitude, and during that time all spontaneity and spirit were eliminated. This wasn't a deliberate policy, but a function of the ambience and general nature of the work. The people around me were sad tedious husks and it seemed that Python was correct after all.

One morning, after a few months, I sat in my chair at work in the morning and came to a sudden realization. I had to go. I had to leave right now or I would go mental. I knocked on the partner's door and was kindly allowed in.

"Hello Kingsley. What's up?"

Julian Dorry still had high hopes that I would come through and eventually become a valuable member of the team. He invited me to sit down.

"Mr. Dorry, I have to go. I mean resign. It's really not for me, this lark. I'm sorry. So I do. I mean resign. Now."

He looked a bit surprised, which in turn surprised me. Surely it was clear to everyone that an accountant I was not.

"Oh. Are you sure? Perhaps you haven't given it a proper crack of the whip."

"I'm sure. Thank you."

When I left the building I felt as though I had just been released from prison. I was on the outside again. A dark cloud had been lifted from my life. The only thing I had got out of my sad office experience was some money, and a fair portion of that went to the seriously depleted Jumble fund.

Chapter 16

KC
The Channel!

In 1989, Tim, Bill, Susan and I decided to do the Big One. No, not a world circumnavigation but something just as daunting for us ocean neophytes. We were going to finally break away from the bosom of the shore and cross the English Channel to Jersey. Jersey, home of the cow and sweater, was 100 miles almost due south from Poole and our journey would take us over some of the most treacherous sailing waters in the world.

The aim was to escape society and sail off to distant lands absorbing life and the world much more richly than could possibly be achieved when chained to a job and family on land. Families could wait, as could 'real' jobs. Jumble was to be the vehicle and here we were testing her out in the Channel in preparation for the first big voyage to Spain, the Azores, and beyond…

None of us had crossed the channel before. Bill and Susan had precious little sailing experience and Tim and I had never been in charge of our own destiny at sea, except for the recent Exmouth voyage. We had Patrick with us then, and he was reasonably experienced navigation-wise. Anyway, the Channel was a big step up from coastal hopping. Although we had sailed on big boats (as opposed to dinghies) a few times, racing around Jersey, there was always at least one person on board who was an experienced navigator. We just crewed and sometimes took over the helming, relieving everyone from the usually appalling 'skills' of the owner. Boat owners often think they are good at steering whereas the truth is that they are simply good at providing a boat for the rest of the crew. Almost always they are frequently luffing and then seem surprised when the rest of the fleet disappears rapidly over the horizon.

Bill and Susan were one up on Tim and myself since they had done a RYA land navigation course and were in a position to recognize, at the very least, the nature of things like cardinal marks and what a Decca positioning system was all about.

We could just see Jumble bobbing about on her mooring at Baiter in Poole harbour. She was about 200 feet away and there was a 5 knot onshore breeze where we were standing. We had quite a lot of kit, 4 or 5 bags of clothes, sleeping bags, food, water etc. Our second hand Avon inflatable was just big enough for three people plus gear, so there would have to be at least 2 trips. The problem was that we didn't have an outboard engine for the tender so one of us would have to row. Bill, Susan and Tim went out first and it seemed to take an age for them to get to the boat. Finally Tim came back and we loaded everything else into the tender. Since we couldn't row properly, we each took an oar and positioned ourselves on either side of the boat and began paddling. I noticed the wind was getting up a bit and progress was getting slower with the wavelets becoming big enough to breach the 2 inch freeboard of the inflatable. Every time we stopped to take a breather, the wind would push us back a few feet and it was becoming a slog. The slightest difference in paddle speed would result in the boat turning round and we began to shout at each other to speed up or slow down. We were paddling seriously hard now and making very slow progress with absolutely no chance of a rest. What I have described was a fairly standard Jumble tender journey.

On board the others were stowing their belongings in the port hull. There are 4 berths on Jumble, 2 in each hull, one forward and one towards the stern. They are all like narrow coffins. The port hull also has the kitchen or galley as you're supposed to say at sea. The cooker was a 2 burner gas affair which had been wedged into place. Underneath in a hodge-podge of shelves were the cutlery, plates, cups and gas canister. On either side were narrow shelves full of, and in no particular order, tea, coffee, tins, matches, biscuits etc. All this stuff was held in place by large quantities of elasticated netting. This netting was almost as useful as the sails themselves and seemed to have a practically limitless capacity for storage. Everything was shoved into the netting; toothpaste, shoes, torches, food, books, pillows. Tim and I had the starboard hull, the entrance to which doubled as the chartroom and tool room. The chart table was positioned right above my head as I lay in my bunk, and theoretically was moveable. In reality there was nowhere else to put it. I could, with difficulty, squeeze into my coffin with it in place.

Each berth was about seven feet long and two and a half feet wide at the entrance (head) end, and maybe one and a half at the other (foot) end. There was just enough room to squash your duffle bag down by your feet and anything else you brought along would have to be efficiently arranged around your head. Coats, pullovers, torches etc. A torch was an essential item as our hull lacked lighting except for a tiny bulb which was held inside a wire stretched across the entrance to Tim's bunk. It gave out just enough light to read as long as you held the book up quite close.

The tool room wasn't a room at all; it was a wooden box-come-shelf about 1 foot by 5 inches deep and 6 inches high. Anything that could be remotely classed as a tool was put in it and much more besides. Fishing tackle, old tins, nails, screws. Finding anything in the box was an irritating exercise because what you wanted was never visible, never even near the top, and when located (by removing a large portion of the contents) always seemed to be connected in some mysterious way to other tools. Everything got rusty within days of being aboard and this accounted for the fact that all the tools were items that had been discarded, and thus were rubbish, in the first place. Now they were rubbish and rusty. Our screwdrivers were all rounded at the useful end. Chisels were those ones which had been used at home as cold chisels and/or screwdrivers, and the pliers were the ones which had been left outside in the rain and now required the strength of a Titan to even slightly open.

Strangely, Tim and I hadn't sailed with Bill and Susan before and it was going to be interesting to see how we all got on. There was no 'skipper' as such since none of us had that much more channel crossing experience than anyone else, i.e. none, and we all owned a quarter of the boat. If anyone had a claim it was Tim because this was really his boat and we all knew it. I think we all agreed that decisions would be sort of democratic with perhaps Tim having the final say in the event of any disagreement. That's how I viewed it. Bill in fact had very little sailing experience, and Susan, zero.

It was about 7 p.m. and we reconvened on deck. Tim brought the charts along and we planned our passage. Actually, there wasn't much to plan, at least not for the first 60 miles. Alderney and the Cherbourg peninsula were about 60 miles due south from Poole and at 4 knots it would take us 15 hours to cross the channel. The tide went east-west so would probably even out over the passage. If we left in an hour or so we would be over there by 11 the next morning with plenty of light to see Alderney. The idea was to get to Alderney and then decide what to do then. Either put into Braye harbour or go through the fabled Alderney Race and onwards south to Jersey. The plan was to leave that very night. It is usual to inform the local harbourmaster of one's passage intentions and this entails talking to him over a VHF radio. This was clearly the domain of Bill (Bill had done, to supplement his earth-bound yacht master's course, a course in VHF radio which left him, we thought, in a superior position to the rest of us as regards communication with the outside world.) He went down into the communications area (also the chartroom, tool room, and part of Tim's bunk) and turned on the radio. We all got our heads into the hull as close as we could to follow proceedings. After all, we may learn something. Bill began confidently
"Poole Harbourmaster, Poole Harbourmaster, this is Yacht Jumble, Yacht Jumble.. Over."
No reply. He repeated it. Nothing. Concluding that the harbourmaster hadn't heard him properly, Bill decided to use some of his specialist knowledge
"Poole Harbourmaster, this is Yacht Jumble. J for........"
There was an uncomfortable pause as he tried to pluck the phonetic alphabet code for J out of his brain, which under the pressure of the moment was escaping him.

"J for, for, January. U for, er, Umbrella, Umbrella. M for Mother, B for um, er, Big Big..."

And then the harbourmaster broke in, putting our expert out of his misery

"Harbourmaster to Yacht Jumble. That's fine thank you. Where are you going?"

Bill wiped away the beads of perspiration that had developed on his forehead.

"Yacht Jumble to Harbourmaster. We are going to Jersey tonight."

"Yacht Jumble. Thank you. Have a good trip."

It seemed that, in an emergency, one of us could perhaps substitute for Bill on the radio after all.

Getting out to sea was pretty uneventful with no last minute catastrophes and I was very excited about the whole affair. I turned to Tim, who was on the helm.

"Tim, this is finally it. Crossing the Channel in your own boat. What do you think about that?"

"It's all our boat King," Bill reminded me. I ignored him.

""Tim. Well?"

"Fabulous. I've waited a long time to do this. Let's hope we don't hit any ships. We should sort out the watches now."

"Yes" said Bill. He continued

"I think that either Tim or I should be on deck at all times for safety's sake."

I almost choked on my hot chocolate. Cheeky bugger! I wanted to punch him there and then. Just because he had done a bit of painting and screwed in a few screws he thought that he was the co-skipper. I had done tons more sailing than him and there he was, on the strength of a shore based 'yachtmaster's' course, relegating me to the level of the ship's boy! I had to say something.

"What do you mean Bill? Are you implying that I, who has a huge amount more sailing experience than you, cannot take watch?"

I wanted to say so much more but held my tongue. I couldn't let this get out of hand. But the damage had been done and I was really pissed off with him.

"No King, not at all."

The ships' crew had now been polarized, in my mind at least. Before it was the brothers and the couple. For me now it was definitely 'The Brothers' vs 'The Couple'. I don't know what Tim thought. Probably nothing since he has a fairly thick skin about these things. I couldn't bear to do a watch with Bill now, and, by association, Susan too. So it was decided that Tim and I would do the first one until 2 a.m.

The wind was force 2/3 westerly and we were clipping along at 4 knots. The sea was slight. It was 11:30 p.m. and I guessed by now that the Couple were asleep. Still seething, I wanted to ease the pressure.

"Tim. What did you think of Bill's comment?"

"What comment?" he said. What do mean 'what comment' - it was out there in red and underlined!

"You know. Bill saying that either he or you should be on deck at all times for safety's sake."

"Oh? Did he say that? I shouldn't worry about it."

As I thought. Not the supportive 'Yes, what does he know' reply I wanted but 'stop fretting over silly stuff'. Nevertheless I had to get some of it out of my system.

"It was a bit rich. He knows absolutely sod all about sailing! What made him say such a stupid thing? Idiot."

"King, just forget about it. Look, he's a nervous sort, you know that."

This didn't help. Bill was Tim's friend from University days and I got the impression that Bill looked up to him, really admired Tim. They had both done a teacher training course together and whilst Bill carried on to actually be a teacher, poor bastard, Tim escaped and did something interesting. Perhaps that was it; Bill admired Tim for not becoming institutionalised whereas he had failed. I was Tim's younger brother, and, as it is often assumed for younger brothers, knew and possessed, in terms of talent wit etc, half as much as the older brother. Thus in Bill's eyes I was the incompetent, always dependent, younger brother.

"So do you think we will get across the Atlantic on this thing?" I asked Tim.

"King! This thing! She's called Jumble. And yes. There is a fairly good chance that we will. This is her major testing out voyage and I have every confidence that she will come through with flying colours."

The big advantage Tim has over almost everybody else is his unbounded optimism and belief that all will be well. He brushes aside all worries and just goes for it without any concern for dangers or potential pitfalls. The amazing thing is that this policy generally works admirably and indeed in Tim's world things do get done; the stuff that should be worried about isn't and in the end doesn't matter! Despite seeing this with Tim over and over again I couldn't help but worry about some of the small things. It;s a curse which my brother is blissfully free from.

For one thing, just how well was Jumble constructed? The hulls themselves were made by someone else, and when Tim bought them he had assumed that they had been made to a high standard. Was this assumption valid? Tim had joined the hulls together with two-by-fours using very large bolts, and then covered everything with epoxy paint. Were the bolts big enough, were there enough of them, and were these crossbeams strong enough?

"Tim, who did you buy the hulls from?"

"The hulls were built by Malcolm, a Suffolk carpenter. His idea was to sail into the blue yonder, but in the end his wife decided they were going to escape to New Zealand instead."

"What was the quality of the carpentry like," I asked.

"Well, Malcolm's skills as a carpenter were evident when I first inspected the beautiful Polynesian lines of the twin hulls. The long curves of the keel supported bulkheads every few feet, top quality marine ply was cold-moulded into place to create the boats sides. Only some of the cladding was incomplete. There were no decks, deck stringers, cabins or hatches. Basically I was buying two big canoes."

It sounded as though the hulls had been made quite well and that anything Tim had done subsequently would not have compromised their integrity too much.

"So all you thought you had to do was to cover them with that canvas stuff and paint them with epoxy paint." I said.

"Sort of. In my ignorance I thought I could finish the job in a few months, despite the fact that to get this far had taken Malcolm, a professional carpenter, over eighteen months. Also, in my excitement, I failed to barter and agreed to the asking price. I could already smell the ocean. Malcolm included a large stack of marine ply (which I later realised was worth more than the boat's price on its own), glue and nails."

Then there was the issue of the mast. Tim had hewn it from a forest in Sussex quite recently and, although I know very little about seasoning wood, it occurred to me then, ten miles out at sea, that Tim probably knew as much as me. I thought we should at least cover this point.

"You made this mast from a tree didn't you?"

"Yes King, from a tree. Wooden masts generally come from trees."

"What happened exactly? I mean, how did you actually get the trees - and when."

"I went into the forest, with the permission of the forest ranger, and selected 3 of the truest, straightest trees I could find, and then cut them down with a chainsaw."

"And then?"

"I hauled them out with the aid of ropes and a vehicle. I cut all the branches off on the spot and then tied lots of ropes around the trunks and pulled them out."

"When did you do this?"

"About a month before she was launched. About 2 years ago I suppose. You weren't around when I raised this mast were you? The trees were straight as pokers when I chose them, but after lying in Bill's yard for a few weeks they began to warp a bit. I chose the least warped one."

I was a little alarmed at this confession.

"How warped?"

"A bit like a banana. But I straightened it out all right with the stays."

"So it's under considerable tension one way."

"I suppose so. I hadn't really thought about it."

That's what I mean. No worries. It was getting late, nearly 2 a.m. and time to change the watch. Tim roused Bill and Susan. Up they came, very reluctant and super-tired. Tim and I went into our bunks. The hard bit is to gather the energy to take all the gear off; foul weather clothing, pullovers, shirts, trousers and all. If you don't, then for some reason you don't sleep very well. I was very tired but before I went to sleep was able to dwell on expert Bill one more time. It would be wonderful to be brought up on deck by the terrified Couple as we were feet away from crunching into the superstructure of a tanker, and then calmly rescue us all from the hands of the hopeless fools by quicksilver thinking and seamanship *par excellence*.....

I woke up a bit confused and then remembered I was on a boat in the middle of the Channel. I looked over to Tim's bunk but he was gone. Bill leaned down into the hull,

"Wakey wakey King!"

He smiled happily, his slightly mad eyes barely discernable through his bottle-bottom NHS glasses.

"Hi Bill. Where are we?"

"Not quite sure but probably about 20 or 30 miles from Alderney. Its 8:30 so we didn't make great progress."

First of all I had to get some clothes on which meant I had to find them. They were dotted around the bunk, all slightly wet. Everything gets very damp sooner or later even without being soaked in seawater, since the sweat permeating your clothes absorbs moisture from the air. The area in our hull where you can put your feet so as to stand upright, about 4 foot long by 18 inches wide, was already completely strewn with Wellington boots and waterproofs that had fallen off the hopelessly overloaded coat hooks. I shoved the pile to one side and gently got out of bed, trying to avoid all the sharp corners and jutting out bits that Jumble is well equipped with. It takes days to get to know the locations of all the corners and I was already quite bruised. On deck the rest of the crew was sipping tea out of plastic Batman cups. Tim gave me one and updated me on our progress,

"I can see Alderney. It's roughly due south and 20 miles away. The wind has picked up a little so we should get there in 3 hours or so."

"Well, which way are we going to go around it? Do you want to go into Alderney?" I said.

If you go round the east of the island then it's the fabled Alderney Race, and if you go to the west it's the Casquets. I happened to know that Tim was much afraid of the Casquets, which is a very nasty outcrop of rocks on Alderney's west side. He had this belief, this fear, that if you go within 50 miles of the Casquets then you would be doomed since they would suck you up and dash you into a million fragments. It could be calm elsewhere, but near the Casquets there are always heavy local seas and rainsqualls. I had never seen them, probably for the best.

"I think we should go into Alderney." said Susan.

"Yes, that may be best." agreed Bill.

I went down into the other hull, Bill and Susan's, to see what was for breakfast. A small pile of dirty looking scrambled egg was sitting in the frying pan. I heard Tim say,

"Oh, King. There's some scrambled egg in the pan. We left it for you. I think there's some bread down there too. Can you put the kettle on?"

The kitchen area was, and always was, squalid. A washing up bowl with a shallow amount of warm water filled with bits of food (often scrambled egg) was the centrepiece flanked by the cooker to the left and a small area to the right that was invariably completely full of plates, assorted foods and dirty cutlery. The frying pan, the one with my scrambled egg in it, fitted into the same category as the ship's tools, i.e. house refuse rescued from the rubbish bin.

This was true for all the utensils, plates etc.; large blunt knives, forks with bent prongs, and dented uncleanable saucepans. The frying pan used to be 'non-stick' but had become definitely 'stick' and had accumulated many thin layers of now sterile organic matter which acted as a sort of insulation. I ate the egg, black bits and all, and a piece of white pap bread smeared with margarine that looked like industrial grease. Tim had been responsible for getting some of the food for this trip and he has been known to be somewhat unfussy about his purchases.

Everything he buys has 'economy' labels which is just one small step above dog food. I don't mind 'economy' toilet paper but 'economy' baked beans are, under normal circumstances, barely edible. When you are sailing however, especially on Jumble, all expectations are altered. Any food, prepared in almost any way, is pretty tasty. The scrambled eggs, and the, normally disgusting, white pap bread covered with grease, was pretty tasty. Now I had to light the gas burner for the kettle, no mean task. The problem was the random delay in the flow of gas after the valve had been opened. When to approach the burner with the lighter? The lighter generated only a minute flame so I had to get in really close and wait for the small 'boom!' as the bubble of gas exploded.

I also thought that putting into Alderney would be a good idea, rather than go all the way to Jersey. We were still afloat and nearly across the Channel and so best not overdo it.

"Maybe we should go to Alderney, have a look around and stay the night." I said. Tim wasn't convinced.

"I think we should go for it. We have all day and the tide should be in our favour for the Race."

"Let's decide when we get closer," said Susan.

We agreed on this. I gathered the cups and put some coffee in each one. I was surprised to see that Tim had got real coffee, not 'economy' stuff. On Jumble you don't wash things up unless you really have to, so the Batman cups rarely saw any detergent. If it's the slightest bit windy on a monohull and you are on a close reach or beating, then drinking anything from a mug becomes awkward to say the least. Lumps of fluid keep on popping out due to the combination of the heeled over position of the yacht and the lurching through the waves. On a cat, however, everything is much more genteel and there is no heeling over. One can wander around the deck without too much difficulty and drinking a cup of coffee presents no problems.

Each hull has a hatch cover that opens up and lays flat on the cabin tops. These hatch covers act as tables or seats and places where you put anything that might fall overboard. I put the full mugs of coffee there and went off over to the other hull to look at the ship's log. This is supposed to be a detailed record of each passage that the boat does, and indeed the first few tentative outings in Jumble were carefully described, by Bill and Susan, in painstaking detail, and by Tim and me a little more tersely. Things fell away after that and the latest trip, from Poole to Swanage, was as detailed as a third son's baby book. Left 8 a.m. Tuesday, blank, arrived 6 p.m. Tuesday. There should be hourly additions noting position calculated by bearings or ready reckoning. The weather conditions and how they are changing were supposed to be jotted down. We just did our ready reckoning on deck and kept it in our heads. 'I reckon we are going at about 4 knots judging by the amount of bubbles in our wake. It looks like it might rain in an hour or two judging by that cloud over there. I think in the last 2 hours we have gone 10 miles.'

Sometimes one of us would make an attempt to do the log justice and enter all the correct things. In fact, I began to use it like a diary when I could be bothered to write. The trouble was, when you finally arrived in port, you were usually so knackered that doing something as mentally demanding as writing is put off for another day.

Now we could see the breakwater jutting out below Alderney's main town of Braye. The gap between the Cherbourg Peninsula and Alderney, only about 8 miles wide, was now quite clear and we were moving rapidly towards it. According to the charts the tide in the Race was about half strength moving southwards. Tim was having second thoughts about the Race.

"Well, perhaps we should just put into Alderney for now."

We took some hand bearings on the breakwater, the peninsula and one other conspicuous landmark and tried to find out exactly where we were. Our triangle on the chart was, as usual, quite large. Our 'position' indicated that we needed to change course to head southeast. After about 30 minutes on this tack it was becoming clear that we would not make the harbour. We weren't even sure of where the entrance to the harbour was. Even though on the chart the breakwater looked huge, from where we were it was almost invisible.

"I think we should head up a bit more. As much as we can," I said.

Tim and Susan winched the sails in as far as they would go and now we were beating. Unfortunately Jumble is poor at beating and it's something you don't want to do if it can possibly be avoided. The water was a little choppy and we were beginning to bash through the waves. We were only a few hundred yards from the harbour entrance now but were drifting east at an alarming rate. It was clear that we needed to tack to make it.

"Let's tack," said Tim.

We tried but she just wouldn't go round. Another thing that Jumble is worryingly bad at is tacking. Furiously we backed the yankee and staysail, all to no avail. You have to get it just right, maximum speed and then the tillers put over at the correct speed, then sails backed just so, and the tillers reversed a split second later. All too much for us to get right and we just wallowed pointing into wind, drifting helplessly into the Race and the unknown demons and Charybdis that awaited us there. We were quite close to the shore and getting closer all the time. Tim emerged from the chartroom,

"Over there," he pointed to a point just off a coastal headland not far away "is a reef that stretches out a mile under water. We'll be over it very soon at this rate. Let's abandon Alderney and just go through the Race. It's half tide and should be fine." He looked a little apprehensive.

We were still in irons and I tried to fill the yankee the other way now. Susan swished the rudders back and forward like on a dinghy to try to get the boat pointed south again. Bill was attempting to start the outboard. It was all getting a bit frenetic. Finally I heard the engine burst into life and we slewed round onto the starboard tack again. The engine then of course stopped but it had done its job. As it happened we went over the reef in any case and peering anxiously over the sides, looked for dark underwater objects, not that much could be done about it. We were moving very fast, which wasn't surprising since we were now in the very wide rapids of the Race, and the shore of Alderney disappeared quickly.

"If we can't tack with ease we're doomed," said Tim looking keenly at the overfalls ahead.

At half tide, as long as the wind is not against it, the Race is like gentle cataracts and exhilarating to go through. We went about 6 miles in half an hour, with most of that due to the current. The French coastline was only 5 miles away and it looked decidedly inhospitable with no place to run to in an emergency. Inland we could see the nuclear power station at Cap de la Hague, in the middle of nowhere, as it should be. We emerged out of the Race unscathed and everyone relaxed a bit. Jersey lay 40 miles dead ahead and getting there before dark, 8 hours away, seemed eminently possible. Tim and I relaxed by playing chess, a game at which we were both equally feeble, although Tim is slightly more feeble than me. Bill was incapable of relaxing. It was as though he was on speed all the time. He was worrying about the tacking fiasco,

"I wonder why Jumble didn't tack back there?"

"Cats are notoriously bad at going about Bill," said Tim. "It's the extra drag of having a second hull to turn through the water. I think we simply need to keep our speed up when tacking."

Bill didn't seem to be reassured and went up to look at the twin bows, presumably in an attempt to find a solution to the problem, but any change in Jumble's geometry was going to be difficult. Finally, he returned, looking anxiously into the distance.

Sark drifted past us to starboard and then Herm, the smallest of the Channel Islands. Although it would have been fun to visit these rocky outcrops, we had decided a while back to forge on to Jersey in order to minimize the tacking. We arrived off Rozel harbour at 9 p.m. This time Tim and I were in the strange position of actually having some local knowledge about the area and currents, the rocks etc., since we had lived in Rozel when we were younger. We tied up to a fishing buoy just outside the harbour and used the trusty inflatable to paddle ashore. I phoned Mum and Dad, who lived up the hill, to tell them we had arrived and would they please pick us up. Crossing the Channel wasn't so difficult after all, and we had sailed practically to our parents' doorstep.

Chapter 17

KC

Mutiny

After dossing about in Jersey enjoying the wonderful beaches and parental hospitality we decided to move on. First of all we sailed around to Gorey, a very picturesque village nestling underneath the fabulous mediaeval Mont Orgeuil castle. A large percentage of the postcards and advertising material produced by Jersey Tourism have Mont Orgeuil and its village as the main visual attraction. We brought the boat right up close to the shore at Gorey beach, a benefit of its very shallow 2 foot draught, and anchored. I thought we added to the idyllic picture, giving it an almost Caribbean feel. We waded ashore, a little cocky. With Jumble, you cannot really be too pretentious because she looks like an up scaled raft. Across the sea from Gorey is Carteret, a small French fishing port, about 15 miles away. We had a westerly wind with blue skies set for the next couple of days and Carteret was a suitable destination.

Tim and I studied the Admiralty chart of the area on the beach and tried to get acquainted with all the data before us. Bill studied the relevant bit of Reed's Nautical Almanac to see if there were any critical pieces of information we should know about. Things like 'Carteret is a very awkward approach in anything other than a light northerly and it is essential to hold a bearing of 30 degrees from the Fleur cardinal mark, otherwise it is easy to hit the rocks just south of the entrance'. I was most interested in, of course, the submerged obstacles, whatever they may be, cables, shipwrecks, rocks, submarines, that lay between us and Carteret. Naval testing areas were other obstacles to be aware of and avoided if at all possible. The biggest object in our way, by far, was the Echreous, a very large expanse of rocks located 7 miles north-east of Gorey. You could sail there, to the Maitre Isle, which had some houses and a small harbour, but this required some really serious navigation and deep local knowledge. In the future maybe, but not this time.

We left early the next morning with more fresh water, assorted tins of food, and francs. The plates, mugs, cutlery and saucepans had been taken ashore for remedial washing in a dishwasher in an attempt to destroy the resident pathogens. All seemed to be well with the Brothers getting on with the Couple, although before we had reached Jersey certain things about them were beginning to irritate me. One thing was the usage of nautical terms. If it had been up to me, sailing jargon would have been forbidden. Susan used words like 'leech' and 'clew' referring to parts of the sail which neither Tim nor I understood, and never would. I even felt a little uncomfortable with bow and stern. Front and back, left and right were perfectly reasonable as orientation indicators. There would be 'lanyards', 'transoms' and pintles', whereas 'bits of rope' holding the wires to the deck, 'piece of wood' at the stern, and 'hinges' were eminently acceptable and universally understood substitutes. Bill was as bad and I could only surmise that they had read too many technical boating articles. Maybe it gave them a comforting illusion of competence. It was also possible that they were trying to gain the upper hand over me by appearing more knowledgeable. Tim even suggested, lightheartedly, that we dispense with the jargon but I think it was taken as a criticism.

It was likely that we were also pissing them off, perhaps by not knowing what a 'clew' was. Tim and I were in general quite slovenly, as indeed was Bill, but this was not true of Susan. She liked things shipshape and was constantly carefully coiling up ropes that hadn't been used for five minutes, into elaborate spirals. Other ropes would be tidied up by folding into 'shanks' that I could never undo in a hurry, which was really very annoying. In truth it was a good idea not to let any ends dangle into the water and foul the propeller, but what was wrong with loose piles of rope?

The sailing was excellent. The sea was smooth and the sun shining which allowed for reading and sunbathing. I found a comfortable spot by the inflatable up at the front on the left and read my book in peace, intermittently snoozing. At certain points of the trip each of us would practice getting a fix with the handheld compass and mark the chart with Jumble's position. I myself became very confident in fixing our position in these almost perfect weather conditions, with fantastic visibility and clear landmarks all around. It also helped that we knew where we were just by looking around. Deep down, well perhaps not that deep down, I knew it would be a different story with poor visibility and rough seas and that we would probably get lost. Nevertheless, I had convinced myself that my navigational abilities were top notch.

After about 2 hours, having avoided all the rocks, we were ready to make an entrance into Carteret. The harbour has a concrete sill across the mouth to hold water back in the marina and thus keep boats floating at low tide. You could, therefore, only enter 2 hours either side of high water. Bill had calculated that we would get there with about an hour to spare but as we got closer it was becoming apparent that the tide was lower than we had expected. Bill had made an error somewhere.

"I'm not sure we will make it over the bar Bill," I said smugly.

"We had better reduce sail and creep up to it. The water does look low." he said, worried. We reduced sail until only the mainsail was up. The idea was to make a grand entry under sail for the benefit of the locals who were watching, but now I was beginning to think that having an engine running would be prudent. Up we drifted until, only a few metres away, Tim, who was at the bow peering into the water, exclaimed he could see the bar and that we would make it. Tim's eternal optimism was a cause for concern and I tensed up waiting for the crunch of the hulls on hard stuff as we glided over the, now clearly visible, sinister concrete structure a couple of feet right underneath us. Nothing. We got away with it.

I was actually having a nap before going off into Carteret to find somewhere to eat when the altercation started. I awoke to Susan's raised voice and it was clear that she was really pissed off about something. The something was Tim.

"Tim, why don't you ever do the washing up? The rest of us do our bit, but you never lift a finger." I didn't much care for confrontations but this one was going to be interesting. Tim came up out of his hull.

"What's the problem Susan?"

"You are. You never do the washing up. We all have to pull our weight you know. It's a chore but we should all take it in turns." said Susan, angrily. This boiling over of emotion took Tim, and me, completely by surprise. Bill and I also emerged on deck. I actually knew Tim's position on this one because I knew Tim; sailing on Jumble, sailing on anything, was not about washing up the dishes. Washing up was a detail and would get done at some point. Getting all sweaty about who should do it and when it should be done diminished the whole purpose of sailing away in the first place. Tim retaliated.

"What? I didn't spend months and years of my life building Jumble to worry about who should be washing up when I'm finally sailing on her. Screw that! Anyway, I *do* do the washing up." Bill, seeing his precious partner under attack clearly knew on which side his bread was buttered.

"Tim, Susan is right you know. You don't really do any of the washing up. It's not fair that the rest of us have to do your work too." I thought Tim was going to explode. If he had had magic powers, he would certainly have made the Couple disappear there and then. I felt that it was a bit rich of Bill, since he lived, by his own choosing, in the most squalid third world conditions in his Wimborne squat. It was time to show where my loyalties lay.

"Come on now Bill. I don't do the washing up any more frequently than Tim, or you for that matter. It's really very silly to argue about this." I fear, though, that the die had been cast. Tim was fuming.

"If Susan finds the conditions on Jumble not to her liking she can always leave. No one forced her to come. That goes for you too Bill."

"Right. OK Tim, if that's the way you want it. You forget that Susan and I own half of Jumble too. Let's sell the boat." It had all got completely out of hand. Tim's fund-raising method had come back to bite him.

"Fine. Let's sell it," said Tim. Everyone was quiet for about 5 minutes, digesting the turn of events. Of course, we wouldn't sell the boat. For one thing, nobody would buy it. Wharram catamarans are a special breed of craft, one which generally has a low second hand price tag. Almost everyone who is in the market to buy a sailing boat knows that Wharram cats are homemade: That they are built not by professional boat builders, even ones doing it in their spare time in their back gardens, but by amateurs in *their* back gardens.

The general course of events is that some ambitious person who wants to go sailing to Polynesia finds that, on inspection, they are poor. This means they are not in a position to buy a brand new yacht and make preparations for the voyage to Polynesia straight away. They initially look in the back of the yachting magazines hoping to find a real bargain in the shape of a fine ocean going yacht for under a grand. Not finding this, they discover that it is possible to get plans and build your own vessel. Initial calculations indicate only a modest outlay of cash is needed. The plans are purchased and the person, who usually has a great deal of enthusiasm and some DIY ability, begins to build the boat, almost always a Wharram catamaran. Despite the simplicity of the Wharram designs, progress is very slow, the cost mounts up, as it always does, and the vessel is now on an asymptotic path to completion. After 2 or 3 years our intrepid amateur's seemingly unbounded enthusiasm for the project is now depleted and the unfinished hulls remain in the garden under a tattered tarpaulin, waiting to be sold, the Pacific islands now forgotten. Someone like Tim buys these hulls and the plans for a pittance and then attempts to get the boat finished and in the water and maybe, just maybe, to Polynesia......

Even if the boat is finished and well constructed, the feeling is that it's homemade and unsafe. In fact, the opposite is often true, i.e. Wharrams are frequently more seaworthy than production boats. This is because Wharram builders overdo it and build them like tanks. Tim was no exception. An example is the way the perspex is installed into the cabin sides. A thousand small bolts were used for each window and, together with the gun-metal paint sploshed around them, gave the cabins the appearance of some strange military vessel, like an unusual WW2 German auxiliary craft.

I couldn't bear the dark and dismal atmosphere any more,
"There wouldn't be any point trying to sell the boat. It's worth a lot more to us than anybody else. Maybe Tim and I can buy you two out." Bill clearly didn't want to withdraw from the whole venture since he liked

sailing on Jumble, and I believe liked sailing with the Brothers, at the very least with Tim. Although I had now made up my mind to minimize the sailing with Susan in future in the light of this ludicrous outburst, Bill was quite like Tim and me, had put a lot of effort into Jumble, and was a reasonable shipmate. I could even forgive him his error of insulting my seafaring abilities, by putting it down to nervousness. It was Tim who defused the situation.

"Maybe this is getting a bit heated. Look, if I do the washing up now perhaps we can forget about this episode."

As is often the case with conciliatory gestures, this one was taken up greedily by the Couple and all was well in a few minutes. Helped by some red wine we were soon laughing, already reminiscing about now legendary (to us at least) Jumble sailing experiences. The washing up problem was to be solved by a switch from real plates to paper ones, which was totally at odds with Jumble's eco-friendly message. Despite the bonhomie, we all knew that something had changed between us. We knew that Susan had made a mistake and it was doubtful that this particular permutation of crew would grace Jumble's decks again after the trip was over. The washing up wasn't mentioned again, and Bill had some thinking to do.

Nevertheless, we still had to sail back to England and at least get on with each other until then.

Chapter 18

KC

The Wave

It was fairly good weather when we left Carteret the next morning and we sped on towards Alderney again. This time we left the Ecrehous to port and sailed close to the French coast. The 6:00 a.m. shipping forecast indicated that the Channel region would be Westerly force 4 to 5, gusting 6. A bit heavy I thought, but no reason not to forge on. It was very wet and each of us retired below deck in turn to get kitted out with warm clothes, foul weather gear and safety harnesses. We had arranged two wire jackstays to run along each side of the deck and could attach our harnesses anywhere along their length. The rule was rigorously enforced that we should always be clipped on. In rough seas, even in broad daylight, it was debatable if we could have turned around to rescue someone who had fallen overboard. After we had been sailing for about an hour, I drew a crude fix on the chart which showed Jumble to be 7 miles Northwest of Carteret and several miles east of the Ecrehous.

Then the weather took a turn for the worse and visibility dropped to a mile or so. The wind increased to at least force 7 and the sea became uncomfortably rough. Jumble was thundering along at a good 8-10 knots and we reduced sail, with some difficulty, to half-furled yankee and a reef in the mainsail. Our speed didn't seem to be affected by this. Then the sun went away and it started to rain. The mood of the crew changed from one of cautious humour and jolly repartee to one of grim seriousness. Within a few minutes it had become the sort of weather that, when on land, you joke about 'not wanting to be at sea in that'. Well, we were at sea in 'that' and to be blunt, it was becoming scary. Tim was maintaining a calm exterior, casually leaving his foul-weather jacket unzipped until a large offering of green water found him. After an hour of thrashing through the water on a northerly bearing we began to wonder where we were. There was no land in sight, even though the coast of France could not have been more than a few miles away. Tim was concerned that we were getting a bit close to Alderney which should have been safely north of us. We tacked back towards France and then after 30 minutes worried that we would hit France and tacked again. This continued, with the time between each tack getting shorter and shorter. Visibility was now less than a mile and, since we had absolutely no confidence in our ready reckoning, we were lost, for the first time ever. As if this wasn't enough, the sea grew even larger and the boat was fairly hurtling down into the troughs with waves threatening to break over our stern. One particularly large wave reared up behind us and Jumble went sliding down it at an alarming angle. It was a shocking feeling as I looked down that wave. There appeared to be a hole at the bottom of the trough where we would surely plummet, spearing it with the two bows almost perpendicular to the water. Time seemed to slow down and I had plenty of it to look round at the others. They were also staring downwards, transfixed by the abyss awaiting us.

How could this come to pass, I thought, that we were apparently about to die a miserable death in the heartless English Channel?

So it was that, in the space of sea between Jersey, France and Alderney, the crew of Jumble became united for a while by The Wave.

As we got closer to the 'hole' it seemed to change shape and, although she hit the bottom with a jarring thud, Jumble slid around it and bounded on. I knew then that the boat would not break up on us whatever happened, and that Tim had inserted enough bolts into the crossbeams after all. After The Wave things seemed to get better and almost immediately the clouds parted and the sun shone through. There, in all its glory, about a mile to the north, Alderney appeared. It was a bit close for comfort, but a fabulously welcome sight nonetheless.

We decided to go to Omonville, a very small port tucked in underneath the Cherbourg peninsula, and do the return channel trip the next day. That evening we went out for a meal to the only restaurant in town. We were all super hungry and very tired. Tim and I chose fish but Susan and Bill had to struggle with the vegetarian dishes on the menu. They were die-hard vegetarians, but The Wave must have done something to Bill's brain because he, clearly after some internal struggle, picked fish too. All those years of tofu and lentils had obviously been a strain and I could only surmise that the transcendental experience of The Wave had released him from his self-imposed prison, if only for this one night. Susan was disgusted. For her it amounted to betrayal.

"Bill! You're not going to eat meat! What are you thinking?"

"Well, it's fish Susan," said Bill, adopting the position of many 'vegetarians'. Susan went through the standard arguments but Bill wasn't really listening. He wanted his fish.

I was quite pleased, as you usually are when someone who has rigorously held a view contrary to yours, breaks down. Also, Bill had moved over a little bit to the Brothers' side of the table so to speak, which was satisfying. Actually, Tim and I were quite amazed at Bill. It was as though he had decided, that night, he was going to start smoking having never done it before. It would have been just as surprising if he had divulged to us that he had become a born-again Christian, or a Jehovah's Witness, or even a conversion to religious fundamentalism of some obscure creed. There he was though, happily munching on some fleshy flounder.

Chapter 19

TC
CAPTAINS

Some achieve command of a vessel through merit, qualification and experience. Other become owners of a boat and thrust command upon themselves. This doesn't always work out for the best. The transformation from sensible, demur, tolerant member of the community to psychotic, paranoid, power-crazy lunatic can be sudden and shocking. More often than not it is the wife who has to experience the full shock of this behaviour change.

The once charming husband suddenly feels compelled to shout and scream instructions. Usually this occurs in stressful situations; maybe the wife has been sent up to the foredeck to clear a tangle in the roller reefing line. She realises that she cannot do it without releasing the tension in the line, but as she returns towards the cabin he starts to yell (usually into the teeth of the wind so she can't hear him anyway).
"What are you doing? It's still not free...GO BACK!"
She tries to explain.
"But you need to undo it..."

He stands, imperious, at the helm bellowing an evermore incoherent deluge of unfulfillable commands. This exchange inevitably ends in tears, mutiny, divorce, exchange of blows, The Courts, etc.

A petulant skipper can render a voyage exceedingly miserable. This maybe explains why all around the world there are solo sailors who remain just that, solo. Intolerable to sail with, and alone because only they can suffer the stream of commands that flow forth from their heads. An enduring misconception is that possession of a lovely boat will attract a lovely partner. Unfortunately, someone single minded and obsessive enough to go off sailing on their own boat, is likely to have some serious fault.

Obviously there are times when an executive decision has to be made in order to remain safe, but these are few and far between.

Virtually always it is possible to come to a consensus on what needs to be done. This is much the best way to go sailing.

The command structure on board Jumble was run along these anarcho-syndicalist lines. If you were awake, and on the helm, you were in charge. There was an unsaid agreement about who pulled in the sheets, attempted making a hot drink, and tried to work out where we were. It was anyone who felt most capable. Each according to their skills, each according to their needs. It was, in fact, a Marxist boat. Like all Utopian systems it had its weak points —like who did the washing up, but on the whole it worked surprisingly well. I suppose it was run more along Trotsky lines where all functioning crew were members of the Party, whilst the Leninists would have an elite group leading the boat to Freedom, only handing over executive command in the event of Paradise being reached.

Outboard Motor Trials

Cheap second hand outboard motors are easily come by, and this is because old outboard motors are notoriously unreliable. They are like sheep; sometimes they will just die for no obvious reason.

People despair of them, attempt to fix them, then put them up for sale in the local marine auction. At this point others, like Bill, step in and purchase these unloved, non-working engines and attempt to bring them back to life. It's a kind of addiction, with almost religious overtones: sick engines are shown the True Way to Successful Operation.

Bill runs something akin to a motor hospice, a place where ancient motors, or those injured in violent accidents, are encouraged to see out their lives, if not in quiet dignity, then in a courageous rearguard action against the depredations of seawater ingress and electrical anomalies. Those rare engines considered truly beyond hope become donors, their body parts sacrificed to keep others alive. One shed in Bill's collection of sheds was given over in its entirety to these fickle motors. Some sat semi-submerged in oily barrels of water, others were having acid administered by tubes to free up their drainage channels, and still others lay in hundreds of small pieces on operating theatre benches.

Old engines always retain one feature: unreliability. As a result, for our first cross Channel venture, it was seen as necessary to have a back-up engine and an emergency back-up. Each corner of the Wharram seemed to be festooned with outboards, two hung above the back beam and one sat in an offset central pod.

Each engine had its own particular idiosyncrasies, its own strength and weaknesses. There was the extra-long shaft Johnson six horsepower, this had been dismembered down to its tiniest components and reassembled twice in a bid to eradicate an elusive electrical quirk which caused starting failures. These glitches were occasional but made unique by the fact that they only occurred when it was desperately necessary for the engine to start. If there was no stress, no pressing urgency, then the motor would purr into life with the merest flick of the wrist. In other circumstances it would behave like a petulant child, refusing to cooperate in any manner or form.

Then there was the Evinrude 8 horsepower; a heavy brute bolted like a wild animal to its own pod near the middle of the boat. This engine was a grim bully, but wonderfully powerful once in full swing. Unfortunately it took considerable strength to start, and was likely to abruptly cut out if faced with a sudden change in throttle settings. The technique was to stalk it, creep up on the throttle and open it by minute degrees whilst whistling and looking the other way.

Finally there was the emergency reserve; the 1950s, all British, Seagull 3 horse power, complete with original brass tank. It had the look of an engine that had been starved to death and then had various body parts plundered and donated to science. This two-stroke engine was quite unbelievably noisy; each explosion in its single cylinder threatened to be its last; great belches of oily black smoke erupted from its exhaust. Virtually superhuman effort was required to start it; the fuel mixture had to be just so, the throttle open to within a few millimetres of exact parameters. Certain, almost magical, incantations had to be intoned and, if the launch sequence was followed exactly, the engine may erupt into life. It was always a one off event, like an Apollo moon rocket. A failure involved a compulsory two-hour wait. We didn't like to use the engine often because it really seemed that it might rip itself to pieces in a hail of shrapnel, and the safest place was to be right on the bows huddled away from its noise and fury.

The engine set up was truly put to the test a few months later. Returning from Jersey to Poole we were running before a fairly large sea off the Cherbourg Peninsula and decided to put into the little port of Omonville. This fishing town lurked behind its small breakwater in the shadow of imposing granite cliffs. The approach involved flying in on a close reach between clusters of rocks that were periodically smashed by breaking seas. The Almanac suggested heading straight for the cliffs and then, on passing the end of the breakwater, turning right and into the shelter of the harbour. This turning right bit involved us heading directly into the wind, there was no room to tack and so at this point an engine would most definitely be required to reach safety. If the engine failed we would certainly drift back towards the cliffs, our desperately deployed anchor would drag and we would be cast upon the rocks. The boat would be smashed to smithereens and we would all drown.

But, as we were painfully aware, engine ignition was by no means a foregone conclusion. As we closed with the coast the ocean floor rose and so did the following waves. They became monsters. Even with two reefs in the main and just a fraction of genoa unrolled we hurtled down the backs of the waves, at one point our towed log indicated 24 knots before the line snapped.

"Do you think we should turn back?" yelled King above the shrieking wind. We all looked behind us; the waves had suddenly become frightening. There was absolutely no possibility of turning the boat around.

"I think we're committed!" I replied. We all looked back again at the rapidly approach line of surf frothing at the base of the cliffs.

A strategy was swiftly devised.

Bill would take on the Evinrude; in the past he had a good working relationship with this engine. Susan would attempt to conquer the Johnson, and King, also at the stern, would teach the Seagull a lesson it would never forget. I took the helm.

We were now going so fast that it was quite impossible to drop the engines into the water; we would have to wait til we had headed up into the wind and slowed down. The idea was that as soon as one engine fired the other two crew members would abandon their charges, with one rushing to the bows to try and grab the first mooring buoy that came within range, and the other would pull in the sails whist offering moral support to whoever was coaxing an engine. If all failed we would hurl the anchor overboard and make a Mayday call on the radio.

Things didn't go smoothly. The boat thundered down the backside of the final huge wave before the breakwater was reached. Hissing plumes of spray hurtled up from the two rudders as if from fireman's hoses. Then came the moment of no return. I pointed Jumble up into the wind. At the same time everyone threw themselves into a frenzy of engine-starting operations.

Bill snatched back savagely on the starting chord of the Evinrude, this promptly snapped and he disappeared with a cry down the open cabin hatch. King hauled with equal vigour at the Seagull, this violent action saw his elbow catch Susan a solid blow on the nose and she collapsed in a heap, but not before her efforts at the Johnson were rewarded. It had started!

"Get her in the water! Coax her, coax her!!" I implored. King stood frozen for a moment between semi-concussed Susan and the spluttering engine, then with commendable speed he stepped over Susan, apologising, thrust the engine into the sea and opened up the throttle. Jumble began to stagger forward towards the outermost mooring buoy.

Bill staggered back out of the cabin and ran forward to grab hold of the buoy just as the engine quit.

"One day, when we're rich, we'll buy a new engine," I said.

Chapter 20

KC

Back across the Channel...

Wearily I dragged myself out of my coffin and peered out of the hatchway. No sign of Bill and Susan, but Tim was on deck getting the sail ties off the main and yankee.

"Ah, King. Looks like a good day for a Channel crossing!" he said with enthusiasm. I peered into the sky; it was overcast with the threat of rain. Meanwhile, there was a cold wind whipping about my head which induced me to retreat back into the cabin and get some clothes on.

"Looks like it could have been even better, perhaps with some sunshine. Where are the others?" I replied from inside.

"Out getting some bread and cheese for our upcoming crossing."

I put all my togs on including the survival suit and safety harness. The less nausea-inducing manoeuvres inside the cabin at sea the better. I helped Tim get the mainsail up. Soon enough Bill and Susan returned from their shopping expedition.

Leaving Omonville was not too daunting, even for us. It was a straight reach to the northwest. In fact, we didn't even have to worry too much about tides since we were just far enough north of the Race to avoid the really strong currents. Anyway, the tide was in our favour. All we had to do was head north. About 4 miles out we passed very close by a ferry, within a few hundred feet. A gaggle of passengers on the top deck outside stared at us, some of them clearly surprised to see such a motley crew out at sea. Perhaps they were wondering whether the captain of the ferry should be encouraged to mount some sort of rescue mission.

We pressed on. The sailing was excellent, and for the next 8 hours or so I didn't have to worry about rocks, land or tides, or indeed any combination thereof. I was sitting on the port cabin top scanning the horizon for ships, the only other real hazard, when suddenly there was a loud grating sound, as though a chain was being pulled against a piece of timber. I looked around Jumble for the source of the noise when Bill shouted

"It's the anchor chain! It's slipping overboard!"

Both he and I lunged at the fast disappearing chain, which by now had eased about 20 feet of itself into the channel and was causing considerable drag on the boat. Mercifully the anchor itself was still on deck, but the two of us were unable to pull so much as an inch of the chain back on board, presumably because of the force of water on it. Another thing that didn't help was that it had slipped through the slats which were only just wide enough to allow a link through. Tim put the boat into wind and we all heaved on the chain, dragging it in inch by inch. After it was stowed again and tied down by as many small pieces of ancillary rope as we could find, I attempted to settle my nerves by imagining tying onto a mooring in Poole harbour. Then Bill casually walked up to the mast and gave the wooden wedge at the bottom of the tabernacle a good kick. I looked at this angled infill and began to realize that it was essential for keeping the mast stable. It had come loose.

"Bill, isn't this a bit serious?" I said.

"Yes. We should probably try to lash the shim into place. I don't know how successful that would be since there is a huge force squeezing it out each time the boat moves."

We hurriedly lashed the wedge in place but the mast was clearly still loose at the foot, and the strain on the metal pin linking the mast to the tabernacle must have been considerable. We took turns in periodically kicking this important lump of wood back under the mast. I went to look at the chart to see how far we had to go and deduced, as far as one could from the thatch of pencil crosses, that we were about 15 miles from the Dorset coast.

The visibility was becoming worse and we couldn't take a fix because we couldn't see any landmarks, or indeed any land at all. In fact the last fix had been a few hours ago when we could still distantly make out Alderney. We had figured out where we were purely on ready reckoning. This meant that our position was accurate to within about 5 miles, which was unacceptable. What were we going to do?

Bill announced that he might be able to use the Decca position finder. I guessed that this must have been one of the skills he had learned on his yachtmaster's course. Could it be that some of this knowledge may actually prove to be useful? Bill tried to explain the procedure to Tim and me. He said there were radio transmitters dotted around the coast of England, each of which transmitted a unique signal in a broad arc.

"What you have to do is scan across the coast with this," and he pointed to a sort of large microphone-like device on the VHF radio. He continued, with us listening in rapt attention.

"You turn the dial on the radio to channel 20 and listen for the telltale signature of the transmitter you expect to be there. The idea is that you then find at least one more transmitter further along the coast, draw lines on the chart according to the bearings of the signals, and we are where the lines intersect."

"Bill, you appear to be talking in riddles, but let's give it a go," said Tim.

Bill took the device on deck, steadied himself against the mast, and began to work his magic. As he slowly swept the horizon, we huddled by him trying to distinguish a signal from the background of hiss. At a certain point a faint hum came from the radio which got louder and then faded away as he moved the 'microphone' slowly in an arc.

"There. Hear that? I think that's one of them," he said excitedly.

He noted the bearing using the handheld compass and went down below to plot the position of the bearing of the transmitter, or the one he thought it was, on the chart.

He took an old-fashioned pair of compasses and marked out arcs, using the transmitter he had located on the chart as the centre, at different distances. In our eyes he began to take on the aura of Merlin and we quickly cleared his path as he reemerged to do more sweeps with the VHF contraption. It was as though he were a time traveller who had come to an earlier, more primitive age, and we were the natives, astounded at the 'magic' we were witnessing. More mysterious arcs were drawn on the chart and then curious intersecting lines. I half expected him to scribe a symbolic version of Kepler's 'symphony of the spheres' in the corner of the chart, or perhaps a Druidical pentagram. Bill, now the High Priest of Navigation, finally and triumphantly drew a circle on the chart and declared it as our position.

Whether or not that circle in reality marked the spot where Jumble was at that moment didn't matter because, for a brief period before we actually saw land, Tim, Susan and I believed it to be true, and that was all the reassurance we needed. Bill appeared to believe it too since he was wearing a very smug expression. After about an hour using the fix as a ready reckoning point Tim sighted land, and in a short while he was able to take a manual fix using the handheld compass. This horizontal compass is similar in appearance to an early version of a Star Trek phaser. The idea is that you point it at a known landmark, a chimney, headland etc., wait for the needle to settle down, and then pull the trigger to fix the needle in place. Unfortunately, the needle never completely settles down due to the motion of the boat, and the bearing could be off by 5 degrees one way or the other. As a result, the fix is error prone and definitely very approximate. Fixes should be taken at regular intervals for the errors to balance out and the track of the boat can then be estimated with reasonable accuracy.

On Jumble, the time between fixes was considerable due to the laziness of the crew. Tim's fix didn't really fit in with Bill's an hour earlier, and it was only when we got close enough to land to see something we recognised, that we really knew our position for sure. Needless to say, both the fixes had been worryingly inaccurate and Bill was immediately demoted from High Priest to lowly follower. We had arrived off the coast by 'Old Harry Rocks', when we thought we should have been 5 miles further east, nearer the Needles. Curiously, later, Dorset landfalls were always at the Old Harry Rocks wherever we thought we were.

We managed to negotiate the chain ferry and sail around Brownsea Island to our mooring in Baiter. After tying off on the buoy we slumped about on the deck very wearily. So we had done it. The mission was to sail the Channel and back in our homemade boat, a feat that a vanishingly small percentage of sailors accomplish. We didn't sink, kill any member of the crew, kill anybody else, or require rescuing.

PART 3

Chapter 21

KC
Hiatus 1990-1995

So, we had conquered the Channel in emphatic style, and Jumble's place in Channel-crossing history was now assured. In retrospect, I suppose it wasn't too surprising that the media was not present at Baiter on our return to Poole. It was a Sunday after all, and the Channel had been traversed by sailing vessels on several occasions prior to our historic crossing. Nonetheless, we had done it the old-fashioned way, using compass and charts and pencils like the ancient mariners, rather than using GPS which is sadly making those old navigational skills rarer and rarer.

Obviously ocean travel was the next target, culminating in cruising around delightful Pacific atolls within the year. Tim and I did not foresee that we were actually going to spend precious little time on Jumble over the next few years, due to a deficit of money and family commitments, which were to a certain extent linked.

Actually, the main problem was time.

Newhaven to Dieppe

When you sail to Dieppe from Newhaven it is usually a good idea to start at about 10 p.m. It's approximately 60 miles, so if you reckon your speed at 5 knots, you will get there 12 hours later, at around 10 the next morning. It's best to arrive in daylight since land is very dangerous stuff. The vast majority of boats that have sunk have hit land. A problem with the above recipe is that it involves sailing at night. On the positive side, there is no land in the English Channel. But you may hit something similar; Ships. The Channel is the busiest shipping lane in the world, bar none. It's a maritime motorway. But I'm much more frightened of real land than ships, so the night passage is the way to go. Don't get me wrong, I'm still afraid of ships. They seem innocuous from a distance; big and lumbering and slow. Compared to an F-16 that's true. Compared to us, though, it's not. Think of it this way, compared to the M1, the Channel is like a rarely used highway, but when vehicles come down that highway they are going at least four times your speed as you try to cross at right angles. What's more is that you actually can't tell exactly how far away the ship is until it's quite close. Then it could be too late. Ships don't change course quickly, mainly because they can't. So you have to change direction, but in a sailing boat that can also be a cumbersome business, especially at night.

So anyway, off we went, Julia, Tim and I just after 10 p.m. on a warm July night. It was blowing a gentle southwesterly. We wanted to go south, so it was fine, a close reach. All crew were in fine spirits, a trip is always exciting no matter how modest. In the grand scheme of sailing things our enterprise was indeed modest, but we were still planning on sailing across the Channel, and for us, that was a reasonably large sized deal. Tim and I had done it several time before, in Jumble, but it's always a little scary. What if something goes wrong? A ship hits us? Lose our way? Just being out of sight of land is exhilarating enough. This was Julia's first time. I don't think she was really that worried, she had not yet grappled with enigmatic tanker lights. Her main concern, which she kept quiet, was the horror of seasickness. She had armed herself, quite literally, with an array of quack wristband remedies which she had presumably persuaded herself were effective. We assured her of their potential success, although I knew they were worthless.

Sea-sickness is not, however, to be taken lightly, and anything that will deter it, no matter how absurd, must be good. We couldn't have one of the crew retching over the side for 10 hours. Desperate. I don't think she was too concerned about her own discomfort, but more that she would be weak in the eyes of the rest of us. She's absolutely right. Others can be ruthless, "oh dear, are you sea-sick?" You glory in your own unseasickness and pity the one who is afflicted. Help is offered to the victim, "Would you like to lie down? Some tea?" The unseasick rush about deck doing things only they can do, rubbing it in.

They only act like this out of a sort of fear themselves - fear that they too could be struck down. I haven't been seasick but can quite see it happening. It's lurking there in the background. Waiting. I cannot stay below for very long, especially in Jumble as it's so cramped. Taking a reading on deck is fine but then going below to plot it in the "chartroom" is quite an ordeal if there's a bit of a swell. You are supposed to do three bearings for a fix, with the boat being in the vicinity of the triangle, but three is sometimes a struggle. Tim has the same problem in rough seas, trying to draw a line on a chart without feeling nauseous, and we have been known to take turns in transferring the bearings.

It was decided that Julia and I would stay up until 2:30 a.m. with Tim sleeping and then he would take over until 6 a.m. We cleared Newhaven breakwater 10:20 p.m. with a bit of help from the trusty outboard, then turned it off, hoisted the sails, the main and yankee, and unfurled the jib. Tim and Julia trimmed the sails as I helmed and then Tim turned in. I said we would only call him if a ship was imminently going to crush us.

Jumble is a little spartan above decks. She comprises two narrow hulls held together by wooden struts with wooden slat decking, making it wet and devoid of seating. The helmsman has the privilege of the use of a small deckchair which slots in quite handily between two of the stern crossbeams. The rest of the crew, on the other hand, which at this moment was Julia, has to make do with leaning against one of the hulls.

It was a lovely evening with a half moon and only a small swell and I felt very content with the world. Then the distant lights started to appear. Local trawlers and other types of fishing boats. Actually they weren't that distant and we gained on them quite quickly. In fact they were stationary. Beyond these boats there was nothing on the horizon, just wavelets dancing about prettily in the moonlight.....

Then we saw the lights. They were small and on our port side, east, on the horizon. Julia took a bearing, as you are supposed to do in these situations. Having done all this before didn't really help me inasmuch as I began to develop a tiny little knot of worry about those lights. It was a ship, no doubt about it. A large one at that. I hoped it would pass in front of us by a good and comfortable margin. I also hoped that it was actually going *very* fast, like a speedboat, so that I could see it would clearly miss us by a very large distance indeed. But it doesn't happen that way. The lights move very slowly and you are kept in a state of anxiety for an unfair amount of time. We plodded along and Julia took another bearing.

"King, it's still 90 degrees"

That's the worst! A constant bearing meant it was heading straight for us. We'd be matchwood within the hour.

"Are you sure?"

Julia took another bearing.

"Well, maybe 95 degrees, it's hard to tell."

Perhaps we would survive after all. Those lights were getting closer and I thought I could make out how they were arranged. Ships are supposed to have one light high on the bridge and another one low on the bow so that you can tell front from back. Sure enough, I could distinguish the sinister arrangement. I comforted myself that if I could discern the lights to be horizontally apart, then it couldn't be heading straight for us. All these worries and calculations when we should have been relaxing and enjoying ourselves.

We were still in sight of land. I wanted the land to go away now so we could be free of the terrestrial world for a few hours. To be completely rid of all those people and houses and cars and noise, in fact to be rid of everything to do with human society. One of the magical things about a boat like Jumble is that it can allow you to do this usually difficult task. I suppose any boat will do the job, even a sailing dinghy, for a short while.

Once Tim and I, when we were teenagers, sailed our Fireball dinghy from Gorey in Jersey to the Echreous, a super dangerous array of rocks about seven miles northeast. To avoid being labelled as being completely foolhardy we went in convoy with a larger cruising catamaran. The trip there was glorious, one of the great moments in Spirit of Zimbabwe's career to go along with a stunning victory in the fast open handicap at the 1984 St. Catherine's sailing club regatta. The Echreous are a bit more than a dangerous bunch of rocks. At high tide there are some crags of dry land with a few houses. Getting to the main island is quite tricky, but we were following the catamaran in front as they picked a route through the submerged outcrop, and for us it was easy (they had to do all the sweating). We stayed for the afternoon until about 5 p.m., when the cat people said they were going back. Tim and I, and one of the cat crew, Paul, decided to hang around a little longer and catch them up later.

The sun was shining and the wind was a force 3 in a very suitable direction. At around 6 p.m. we thought we should sail back. It was summer with a good 3 hours more daylight. The wind was still fine and off we went feeling very comfortable and at one with the world. Jersey was very clear to the southwest, only 7 miles away. We reckoned we would be there in an hour, possibly beating Muscadet, our previous escort. In fact, we were so relaxed that we began a little mackerel fishing.

After about 45 minutes the wind died and the fishing line came in sharpish (with no fish of course). Our mood changed very rapidly from cockiness to anxiety. Jersey was still a couple of miles off and we began to adopt light wind racing measures - minimum movement in the boat except for choreographed caressing of the slightest zephyr that came our way. We were inching towards St. Catherine's bay but we knew now that it would be a close run thing, for the tide was taking us northwards at an ever-increasing lick. We had, by luck, brought the spinnaker with us and decided to put that up, but we were on a close reach and it only just managed to keep its shape. In fact, it generally hung feebly under its own weight due to lack of wind.

The breakwater was inching ever nearer and we could now make out the Fara beacon in the bay, which marked another bunch of rocks that gave me the creeps. Onwards we crawled, aiming to just squeak in between the breakwater and Fara which were separated by perhaps 1000 metres. The current was getting stronger all the time sweeping up past the breakwater which was now generating spooky little whirlpools as water rushed by, like vortices peeling of an aircraft's wingtip. We were now about 500 ft from the breakwater on one side of which was safety, pats on the back, smugness and joyful retellings of our odyssey, and on the other side was fear, more fear, and possible death upon the unforgiving rocks from whence we just came. 200 feet, 100, 50, 25 and there we were on the verge of going to the 'other side', whirlpools and all, when a little breeze popped up and filled the previously sad and drooping spinnaker giving us just enough to slip in on the side of salvation. We were practically up against the granite of the breakwater but mercifully out of the tide and safe.

At this moment, however, we are a long way from that famous breakwater. Indeed we are entering the English Channel shipping lanes. Julia took over helming and I anxiously scrutinized the lights. Closer and closer they came, those lights. Of course I couldn't tell if they were going to go in front of us or behind. How far away? 1000 metres maybe? I can't believe this! It's going to hit us! We could hear the damned engines! I shone a torch up at the sail in a hopeful attempt to get their attention and then said to Julia "I think we should turn round". Of course the correct term is "tack" but in moments of crisis (on Jumble at least) nautical terms tend to be replaced by sensible everyday words that we all understand. The trouble was, if we turned now, it may just slow us up nicely to be exactly on collision course, whereas if we carried on maybe we would be all right.

"Let's get Tim up," I said.

One unexpected problem was my brother's hallucinatory experiences when deprived of even a small amount of sleep. When manning the dog watch he spotted a light which rapidly swelled in his imagination to a large fishing boat, then to a cargo vessel and within a short space of time to a huge passenger liner, possible aircraft carrier on direct collision course with Jumble. His alarm was infectious – Julia imagined she could see the portholes. I was summoned on deck and we all donned lifejackets. Torches were earnestly played on a white sail. Flares were readied, appeals on the radio "Large Liner, Large Liner, this is Yacht Jumble. We appear to be on a collision course, Should we stop, continue, turn around?"

Silence! "You know, I think it's not so big," I said.

Finally we could make out the small white wake and within minutes a 20 foot fishing boat passed a hundred yards in front of us.

Yes, it's true. We did survive that close call. Tim was right about one thing, by 2:30 a.m. I was very very tired and struggling to stay awake. It was fabulous to be relieved of duty so I could go below and squeeze myself into one of Jumble's coffin-like berths. I didn't remove my contact lenses since I would almost certainly have lost one if I had tried the operation. In those days contact lenses were so expensive losing one was practically like losing the eyeball itself. No, better to leave them in despite the danger of them becoming part of the eye by morning.

Chapter 22

KC
Dieppe to Jersey

Well, anyway, we got to Dieppe and Julia left us to return to more urgent things back in Newhaven. To be honest with you I don't remember where we stayed in Dieppe apart from on Jumble of course. Naturally we were in France which meant boulangeries and real croissants in the morning. Despite its raft-like appearance I always felt slightly superior being on Jumble. All the yachties around us on bigger 'better' monohulls had it easy with all the latest gadgets and sophisticated communication devices whereas we had nothing except a VHF radio, and only Julia knew how to operate that. Tim and I had tried, but it was all too much, so many channels and knobs. Eventually Julia explained that you only had to remember one knob, the 'on/off' one, and one channel, channel 16. I knew that in an emergency I could probably get to grips with it. Channel 16. Our electrical system was crude. A single old car battery comprised the heart of it. A couple of wires fed the masthead light and a couple more supplied a charging current from our wind generator. That was it. No other wires at all. One of its greatest advantages was that we could all understand it. Even Tim. When I got back from the boulangerie he was lounging in the deckchair reading a book from the ship's modest library. It was about hardships and great bravery on the high seas. They all were. So what if we haven't battled the Southern Ocean yet? We might, and then knowledge of improvising sea-anchors could come in pretty useful.

We had breakfast and began to plan the next leg; Dieppe to St. Vaast La Hougue, right across the Bay of Seine, the same bay of the D-Day landings. It was 20 miles as the crow flies and with the gentle southerly breeze it should take us about 5 hours. Much to my relief, the Admiralty chart of the area didn't indicate any obstacles such as rocks. There were a couple of wrecks to watch out for, and of course the remains of the Mulberry harbours used in the D-Day landings. Again, we had lovely weather, force 3 southerly, a flat sea, and sunshine. We sped along at a good 4 or 5 knots and I thought, this is fabulous sailing weather and especially fabulous on Jumble. It was, after all, a homemade boat. My contribution to its construction was minimal, a bit of paint here and there, the odd bolt and screw; did I make a hatch cover? No, this was more Tim's handiwork. Jumble didn't sink on her launch. She sails very nicely and today was perfect. No bashing into short sharp waves or stressful gale force winds but a flat sea and 10 knot southerly wind allowing her to skip across the water.

Tim sat comfortably in the deckchair helming by resting a hand on one of Bill's beautiful curved tillers. I had set the sails and lay in the netting at the bow reading Adrift! a story of being shipwrecked off the coast of Africa and drifting thousands of miles in a liferaft. I had got to day 35, the bit when he noticed that his dental fillings and crowns were loosening because his gums were shrinking. About 50ft below us were the rusting carcasses of Allied tanks and landing vessels and the skeletons of men. 135,000 soldiers were landed in 24 hours with about 12,000 casualties with the Germans losing 7,000. 20,000 French civilians were killed, mainly by Allied bombing. One of the British frigates was shelling the German bunkers, which should have been a waste of time since they were many feet thick and almost impenetrable, when at one German gun battery a shell, by an amazing piece of good luck, threaded itself through the main gun slit killing everyone there. A little while later, by a statistical fluke, the same frigate did same thing at another bunker with a similar result. The Germans were spooked by this and, thinking that the British had perfected a new super accurate weapon, left their posts and retreated.

It was 7 p.m. now and we still had 5 miles to go but the wind was getting lighter and the light was fading. No problem, we could see the entrance to the harbour, and so we pointed in that direction. Still 2 miles away the daylight started to go fast and it was becoming apparent that we may have to begin to scrutinize the chart and almanac for any helpful advice. Reeds said there would be a light at the entrance which would strobe in some sort of complicated manner. I got out the binoculars and tried to find it but all I got was a shaky close up of all manner of lights, cars, houses and, well, possibly harbour lights.

Tim announced that he thought he could see the light. Yes, there it was, one flash, wait 2 seconds, 2 quick flashes, wait 5 seconds, one flash. I was less optimistic. It wasn't going to be that easy. We have identified precious few lighthouses by their characteristic patterns of illumination and I saw no reason why this occasion should be any different. I studied Tim's harbour light and concluded that it must have very recently changed its signature to a very eccentric, almost, chaotic strobing since that is what it was doing now. The parallax effect on street lights and moving car lights had conspired to generate Tim's light. Then it was dark and it all became very serious.

We both strained to see the entrance and I was sure I could. The closer we got the less sure I became and then Tim said "Oh no! Rocks!" We tacked as only desperate sailors can and headed back the other way. "Rocks?" I said. "Yes, the entrance must be further south". We felt our way south, our eyes beginning to hurt with all the strain of staring into blackness. Finally we saw the entrance, which turned out to be very small. Tremendously relieved, we went in to the harbour using the Evinrude, only to find a choice of several channels to take. Confused, we just dropped the anchor there and then. A bottle of red wine was produced which, regardless of its origin and vintage, always tasted extremely good at times like these.

In the morning we surveyed our position and motored up to the town centre which was right on the river. Jumble, as always, attracted plenty of attention, a mixture of admiration and aghast. Admiration at the remarkable seamanship of the crew to navigate such a raft even up a river, and aghast at the foolhardiness of even attempting to go to sea in such a raft. After mooring against the main pier, Tim climbed up a nearby ladder and announced our presence to the local French customs person, as is customary when you arrive in a new port. Then we stuffed our pockets full of francs and had a look round town, and talked French to the townspeople.

One problem was that neither of us could speak French despite living almost all our life on an island that was a mere 15 miles from the French mainland. Most of the street names on Jersey are in French. It should be a French island. At school I learnt gargantuan amounts of French and became an expert in irregular verb endings. Despite not understanding even in English concepts such as conditional and future perfect tenses, they held no fear for me in French. But I couldn't actually speak the language. Nobody at school could except perhaps for a couple of French teachers and the boy languages wonder, William Rendle. Other than him, and he was a complete freak, we were all hopelessly inhibited.

When I actually spoke French, especially when a French accent was attempted, I felt absurd. It was humiliating. To pass French O level, at that time a prerequisite for entrance to university, you had to pass the French oral exam. How could this incredible feat be achieved?

To properly highlight our ineptitude a student teacher from France was brought over to, well, talk to us in French. This was a French person who really spoke French. I can remember the moment well. We were all assembled in another room in an informal arrangement. The young French teacher was in the middle and we formed a circle around him. Then the torture began. He picked someone at random, Daryl le Fevre, and asked him a question in French. Daryl looked appalled and really quite scared. There was a pause as he tried to do two things, one understand the question and two, try to remember how to say anything, anything at all, in French. Since he clearly didn't understand what had been said he mumbled "Je ne comprends pas le question" in a terrible English accent.

By the time the Frenchman got to me he had simplified his questions to the bare essentials like "Quel nom as tu?" He was shocked as much as we were at the gravity of the situation. One by one he uncovered our virtually non-existent skills at conversational French, except of course for William Rendle with whom he developed quite a rapport, chatting easily and laughing. All we heard was noise coming out of their mouths.

For the oral exam we had to prepare three topics, any one of which could be used as the subject for the external examiner to talk to us about.

The secret was to pick your topics so that they would overlap by at least 90%. So for William, who was naturally free of this constraint, it would be Pygmies of the Kalahari, the current political state of France and wines of Bordeaux, whereas for me it was my family, our holiday, and our family pet. I was able to condense down the numbers of words and phrases I would need to know to a manageable level since, although the examiner wasn't to know this, my family was actually the core of each topic. On the evil day I was quite nervous. We sat on either side of a desk and he put three cards upside down on the table in front of me, I presumed that they had written on them 'my family' 'our holiday' and 'family pet', and he said something which had to be "pick one". I was so nervous I couldn't find the French for "that one" and so all I could do was point at my choice. What a start. He smiled, turned over the card, and then asked me a question. I ignored it and told him all about my family in a statement I'd prepared earlier.

That night we had a good French meal at St Vaast and discussed the plans for the next day. The idea was to go north up and around the Cherbourg peninsula, then down through the Alderney Race, and past Cap de la Hague leaving Guernsey to the west. We would have to decide what to do as regards where to spend the night later in the afternoon. The weather forecast gave us cloud but the wind was about force 3-4 and if we left early we could catch a fair tide.

Getting the tides right is the key to sailing around the Channel Islands. The English Channel is quite shallow particularly between Alderney and the Cotentin peninsula, at some points being only a few metres deep. This channel is the Alderney Race and the current can reach rates of 10 knots. Obviously you can't fight that in a sailing boat. In the morning it was indeed cloudy and a bit windy. We togged up in foul weather gear and set off under full sail. I wanted to put a reef in the mainsail before we left, but Tim thought I was being a bit of a sap, and then so did I, so no reef.

Sailing up past Barfleur was uneventful, a little choppy perhaps but pleasant sailing. I even practised some navigation taking bearings on various landmarks and etching crosses into the chart. Then we began to round the peninsula and things turned somewhat uncomfortable. The wind got stronger, the waves bigger. It was becoming clear that we were overpowered and that my prophylactic reef would have been a good idea after all.

We attached ourselves to the boat with safety lines, Tim to the rear backstay since he was helming, and I to a cable that ran down the length of the boat. Jumble was lurching horribly now and this was the worst kind of sea for her, all confused waves, some large, some small and we were getting very wet. I began the awkward task of putting a reef in the mainsail. As I loosened the halyard the sail began to flail around with amazing ferocity and I thought "I don't much like this part of sailing". I couldn't get the last reef line tied around the boom because the rope was too bleeding short and the combination of concentrating on this task and the constant jerking around of the boat made me feel nauseous. I had to do some helming right now and shouted at Tim, no doubt amused at my efforts, that it was his turn.

We had just got the reef in when some nasty looking overfalls appeared ahead, much to my chagrin. I don't like overfalls. The tide was running over shallow ground, generating large local waves. From a distance they looked like whitewater river rapids, a large amount of white froth that no one in their right mind would go anywhere near. We wanted to go around them but in no time at all we were in them, up and down crashing through the foam and waves. Then we were clear again. It's all a dangerous business, this sailing lark.

As we rounded the Cherbourg headland Alderney came into view. Tim checked the tide tables again. It was about 1 p.m. and the tide was in our favour going southwest for the next 4 hours. The wind was westerly so the waves in the race would not be too scary. If the wind had been blowing in the opposite direction to the current, especially in full flood, then the race would have been very scary, like an endless tract of overfalls.

So we entered the Race and all was well. As we went further whirlpools began to show up, like at the end of St. Catherine's breakwater, but this time about the size of Jumble. Despite moving over the water at 5 knots the boat was moved around this way and that, sometimes at right angles to our direction of travel as the swirling currents did their thing. On the helm you could not really control the direction using the tiller. After about 30 minutes we were through and the water went back to normal. When I'm on the helm of Jumble and it's a bit rough (or even when it's not) I find it best to stand with one hand on the tiller and the other holding onto the backstay. From there I can anticipate and move together with the boat as it lurches and rolls with the waves. Alderney was receding rapidly to the north and it looked like we were going to make our goal, Jersey. We were approaching the north coast of the island and this meant two sets of rocks; the Paternosters and our old friends Les Ecrehous, came into view. There is a gap of a few miles between them and we decided to head for that gap and then slip inside and hug the coast going eastwards around to Gorey.

Another look at the tide charts and the time showed that we were now being swept quite quickly southeast, 4 knots or so. At this moment one of those miraculous combinations of conditions and emotional state of mind occurred. Under the glorious hot sun, which had now made an appearance, the sea turned aquamarine and flattened out eliminating the jolts of motion, and the wind steadied to a constant force 4. Jumble flew south and I thought 'this is what it's all about – it's why I love sailing!' All the bad sailing experiences are forgotten and the moment seems so perfect and real that everything else pales in comparison.

Then Tim broke the spell by noting how the western-most outcrop of Les Ecrehous was looming alarmingly large. We were now being swept there at over 4 knots judging by the tidal wake against a passing fishing buoy. We bore away slightly to the southwest, gaining speed in the process. I mean, we were racing as it was! Now the anxiety that usually accompanies sailing reappeared. Would we make it? I kept on glancing over to the evil outcrop. At one point we discussed the possibility of going to the east of these rocks but almost immediately dismissed the notion as suicide since there was a whole galaxy of rocks over there that way. Then we were past them all and life was very good again.

We could see Rozel pier and then St Catherine's breakwater came into view. This time it was a pleasure to see the little whirlpools, which were like old friends now, and we waved to the anglers at the end of the wall. Fara beacon looked small and benign now. St.Catherine's bay was glistening, (the site of our early formative sailing experiences in Mirror dinghies,) and the spectacular sight of Gorey Castle appeared round Hell's Corner.

Treacherous reefs abound amongst the Channel Islands, and, to endanger the sailors further, they are set upon by some of the strongest tidal flows in the world. Half the English Channel attempts to get in, and then out, through the narrow gap between Cherbourg and the island of Alderney. If the wind happens to be blowing in the same direction as the tide then the seas don't build, but do swirl in strange whirlpools – all most disconcerting.

Two of the most deadly reefs are called the Paternosters, and the Ecrehous. They sprawl about one mile off the north coast of Jersey, grim, saw-toothed granite jaws. In heavy seas they explode white in sea-foam, like some lathering salivating beast waiting on its rusting restraining chain to gobble you up.

When, in 1870, a group of nuns being transported by fishermen from one convent to another, their boat became impaled on the reef. They were abandoned by their seamen – who headed for shore in a small rowing boat – no doubt assuring the terrified nuns of their imminent return. The nuns, all 38 of them, were left as night came, clinging to the black rocks. The weather fell calm, but this did not prevent the non-swimming nuns from being engulfed by the rising tide and swept, in ones and twos, to their deaths. From the shores of Jersey people could hear them praying and crying in the still night air; and the rocks were named after their final prayers, 'Pater noster'. Boats sent to rescue them arrived too late.

The Ecrehous is an even more extensive reef about two miles east of the Paternosters. At low tide it covers acres. At high tide it is reduced to a couple of islands – and on these a few fishermen' houses cling. In strong winds and big seas no one dares go near. Between the Paternosters and the Ecrehous is a gap, and if you know exactly where, it forms an adequately large passage through. As it was, neither I nor Tim were totally sure of exactly where we were. Jumble thundered on down on a close reach, the sun had begun to set; every fix we took seemed to place us ambiguously either heading directly for the rocks or….. I could hear the wailing of the nuns.

Chapter 23

KC

The Big Theory

Tim thinks that sailing boats have been the key to the advancement of humans over the past 20,000 years. One day, as we were both scraping the barnacles of the bottom of Jumble as she lay on the sand at Gorey Harbour, he divulged this insight to me. I think he must have just reread Kon-Tiki or something similar, since he appeared to be inspired by Thor Heyerdahl's spirit of speculation. His argument went something like this:

Mont Ube. A wild speculative interlude.

Somehow, there has to be a connection between sailing and the origin, or at least advancement, of human culture. The main claim of the thesis is that in order for rapid cultural and technical progress ideas need to be spread from group to group so that, to use a piece of scientific jargon, cooperation can occur between the ideas to generate more ideas. An enzyme is usually made from several subunits, say four. One of the subunits has a small amount of catalytic activity, two of them joined together have more than the sum of two single units, three has more than the sum of three single units and so on. This cooperation gives you the concept that the whole is much greater than the sum of its parts.

Ideas work in the same way. Imagine 50,000 years ago lots of small groups of our ancestors all subsisting as hunter-gatherers. Each group may have had some innovation peculiar to their group. An idea takes a long time to develop and it is unlikely for any one group to produce more than one idea over thousands of years. In the same area the same idea may be independently discovered by several groups since the environment is similar. Nothing is really changed by the sharing of the same idea. The stumbling block is difficulty of exposure to new ideas generated by dissimilar groups of humans that may be far away. This is where sea travel comes in. But, first of all, Mont Ube.

From Gorey Harbour it is only a fifteen minute walk up the hill and then along a couple of narrow lanes to one of the prehistoric wonders of

Jersey, the dolmen at Mont Ube, one of about fifteen such sites on the island. This one is still in very good shape and consists of an oblong ring of large stones. At one end several cross stones have been perched on top of some of the standing stones, similar to Stonehenge. The dolmen is between 6,000 and 10,000 years old which makes it neolithic. From the dolmen you can see the sea, indeed all the dolmens are situated on the coast. One speculation is that they were constructed not just for religious purposes, but also as navigation aids.

"You see King, without sailing boats there could not have been an exchange of ideas between groups. Humans would be no further advanced now than modern chimps, weeding out termites with sticks. In fact, those first sailing boats must have been very similar to a catamaran since it is so stable and can carry a lot of stuff."

Jumble was beginning to change in front of my very eyes, being elevated from cherished homemade vessel to the vehicle of homo sapiens recent rapid rise on Earth. The similarities with Heyerdahl were inescapable; both Thor and Tim (especially Tim) had no real standing in the field of anthropology, both involved sailing boats, and both theories were almost certainly wrong. I brought these minor points to Tim's attention.

"Heyerdahl wasn't necessarily wrong King. It's just that Easter Island was colonized from the west as well as from South America. He would be right back on track if someone could find some DNA in an old Easter Island skeleton that originated from South America."

One of the curious ironies about Easter Island is that the current inhabitants do not want to have originated from South America. Despite Heyerdahl making the place famous, they resented his theories. If you read his book about his amateur excavations on Easter Island in 1959, *Aku Aku*, you realize that the locals were having him on and he wasn't fully aware of it.

"Somehow, I don't think that's very likely. So, what will be our 'Kon Tiki Expedition'? There's not much in the way of reeds round here."

I could hear Tim scraping away. After some thought he said

"I believe that if we can show that primitive man could sail between all the Channel Islands and England on a basic raft, then we have gone a long way to proving my ideas."

"So Jumble is our Kon-Tiki?"

"Yes, absolutely."

Chapter 24

TC
Alderney to Poole

Getting up before dawn leaves me close to delirium, but this was necessary in order to allow Roger, our pilot, to return home in time to get on with the harvesting. We were to fly to Alderney in his light plane, a Jodel. The aircraft looked preposterously small, almost like a rich child's model, the turned-up fabric coated wings glistening with early morning dew. When we arrived at the grass strip Roger was washing down the windscreen with soapy water. I was wondering how on earth we were going to fit in, let alone our two huge sailing bags. It reminded me of hitching in France, the cars that stopped were inevitably packed to the gunnels, but desperation always aided the attempt to cram a full rucksack and oneself into less than 1 m^2.

Roger helped me strap in.

"If I should die, or pass out, you are to take over and safely land us," I was told.

I tried to look positive and competent. I had, after all, read numerous books on Second World War fighter aces. I looked back at Julia who seemed blissfully unaware that we were about to cross the Channel in a toy aircraft and that, in the unlikely event of Roger's sudden death, I was to be her pilot. She clambered in herself and smiled cheerfully as she put on some earphones. I tuned my attention to the controls and eventually identified what was clearly a clock.

Small aircraft vibrate a good deal and, with the throttle opened wide, make a frightening amount of noise. We bumped down the grass strip between the fields of ripe wheat and climbed into the dawn sky.

The south coast of England soon spread out in the hazy early light and I identified Chichester harbour and the various anchorages that we had visited with Jumble. The drone of the Rolls Royce engine was pretty intimidating, even when armed with headphones. It seemed remarkable that there was enough room in the cowling to accommodate such a machine, but strangely comforting. Surely a Rolls Royce wouldn't pack up on us in mid Channel?

But I also remembered that a friend of mine, Mike, had been flying a similar aircraft to my sister's wedding in Jersey when, at 500ft with the coast of France in sight, the engine had stopped. His wife, Nujo, pointed at the still propeller and said something like,

"Mike, do something!"

Mike desperately scanned the controls and said something like,

"Be quiet whilst I try and save our lives!"

He had failed to switch over fuel tanks. This done, the engine restarted, and they made it to Jersey where, arriving unannounced, Nujo was mistaken for a hired maid and put to work in the kitchen and Mike was used as ballast on my dual paraglider.

The Jodel vibrated and whined to the Isle of Wight where we turned towards France. This was the route that involved crossing as little water as possible. Apparently, being made of wood, the Jodel floated pretty well, but looking down at the white caps on the Channel I didn't rate our chances. The flight continued well until Roger informed a terse French Air Traffic Controller that we were about to fly into a restricted danger area. A missile firing zone or the like. This necessitated a sharp turn and loss of height. Shortly afterwards Roger began peering earnestly into the hazy distance, then he casually asked, "Recognise anything anywhere?" Julia pointed out of her side window at a small island. It was Alderney. We were saved.

I could hear in my subconscious a story about a maiden in the valley below. Apparently someone was anxious that she did not leave them, or deceive them. This all seemed very strange as the whole narrative was transmogrified into some insistent piping that I soon realised was coming from the radio. My brain clawed at reality as I tried to open my eyes and then the shipping forecast began.

I lay like a cocooned caterpillar in my coffin bunk on Jumble as she gently bucked on her mooring in Braye Harbour, Alderney. The wind shrieked in the rigging and rain pattered down on the deck. Every now and then there was a dull thump as a wave smashed into the breakwater. About ten seconds later a great plume of sea spray would cascade down on our little catamaran. Were we completely crazy to be here?

Our sea area was attended to by the BBC; wind, west-south-west Force 4-5, occasionally 6, and all this was 'good' according to the announcer. I knew he was referring to the visibility when he said good. But it was difficult to reconcile the howling wind and crashing waves outside with this 'good'. I undertook the wriggling manoeuvre necessary to turn over within the confines of Jumble's bunk, then I hunched up on my elbows and looked over to Julia who was already awake and with that 'are we completely mad' look in her eyes.

"The BBC said it was going to be good", I said just as another great avalanche of seawater drummed down on the boat. She raised her eyebrows. It was clearly time to get the kettle on.

Only the afternoon before we had been dropped off by Roger, the weather had seemed reasonable on arrival. But by the time we had taken the water taxi out to Jumble, rain had begun to fall as heavy cold-front clouds swept in from the Atlantic. During the night it had poured.

A cup of tea works wonders and once I had donned full waterproofs I ventured on deck to prepare. Braye Harbour is semi protected by a mile long granite breakwater, a vast Victorian edifice intended as one half of a harbour for the British Fleet. They built a similar half harbour at St. Catherine in Jersey (the famous breakwater), only for the Napoleonic Wars to end. The Braye breakwater protects you from the northwest, but not from the northeast. We knew that once we put our nose out past the pier's end things would be considerably rougher.

But, half an hour later, with two reefs in the sail, and in full survival suits, this is what we did. We set course for Poole, and hammered into the Channel. After about half an hour a huge rent of blue sky appeared as the back of the cold-front scurried past. Sunshine does marvelous things for the spirits, with Julia on the helm I even shook out the reefs. Jumble was flying along with surf leaping in her wake. The wind moved astern and we decided to put up the spinnaker to see how fast we could go. It was all I could do to trim the Spinnaker and so Julia remained on the helm for what seemed hours!

The wind gradually built up to a Force 5, and we were maintaining over 10 knots. This was wild sailing. Every now and then I would rush below to provide hot drinks and chocolate as we hurtled down wave after wave.

On Jumble any type of sustenance is always gratefully accepted but in general nobody ever cast aspersions on the products of a sea-cook, whomever it may be at the time. This is a universal rule. Anything vaguely edible produced below decks has a value out of proportion to its actual quality. For me there are two fundamental restrictions; firstly the availability of ingredients, and secondly the whole process has to take less than 10 minutes.

Occasionally we would up anchor having failed to reprovision. Tins of, usually, Tesco's asparagus soup, out of date by 6 years, followed by prunes would be relished with peculiar gusto. Presented on red plastic plates, eaten with teaspoons. Plates were polished clean with blocks of stale bread, like Benedictine monks at the end of Lent.

It took us about nine hours to reach Studland Bay (the Old Harry Rocks of course) where, just as the sun set in a red fire, we anchored in glorious triumph.

Chapter 25

TC
Epilogue

It is not too hard to identify the reasons why there isn't a chapter titled "Jumble in Tahiti". Just as we had become quite proficient at sailing our boat and were ready to do at least an ocean passage to the Caribbean, babies started appearing. Our babies.

Thus, in 2005, it has been over 20 years since we launched Jumble. In that time we have raised families and followed unlikely careers. But we still recall with fondness our adventures on the catamaran. Jumble was not really the boat to accommodate little children, at least not for us, and the Polynesian islands would have to wait a bit longer.

She still floats, rather in need of some tender loving care, in the middle of St. Aubin's harbour in Jersey. I haven't actually been on board for a year. The cross beams probably need renewing. That's a mammoth job.

Bill and Susan got married and have two sons, they still sail on an old monohull and Bill is a headmaster, and Susan works in a hospital. Patrick raised his family in Jersey and still sees Jumble from time to time.

Jumble took on a life of her own. People seemed to love the idea of a boat being built in a back garden by penniless adventurers. Loads of people have sailed on her over the years. At our sister Imogen's wedding we sailed all her wedding guests (ranging in age from 2 to 82) around Gorey Bay. She's a lucky boat and will soon set out on adventures again.

As for the idea of escaping from Western civilisation, this has proved more difficult (children, money etc.). For nearly twenty years we have had a cruising catamaran ready in a harbour, we fondly imagined that at some point changed circumstances would see us loading up and sailing off into the blue.

But wait! We now have a new boat, another catamaran, another Wharram, called Bumble Bee awaiting an ocean crossing cruise. This one can take children....

Appendix

TC - Sketches superbly rendered by KC
Building a Wharram Catamaran

To build your own boat is not a task to be undertaken lightly.
Firstly you require almost pathological tenacity, and secondly you will need a large space to build it in and a lot of wood. And glue. These points represent the barest minimum. Each stage can take up to a week or more. Initial enthusiasm can slide to despair on occasion. Having friends around to help, and re-inspire, is vital.

Buy a set of plans. These come as about twenty large sheets. *I spent hours and hours studying plans. They really give only a broad idea, you have to interpret them like a religious text. The plans soon get covered in glue and torn. A good idea would be to laminate them. Sometimes its best to embark on smaller projects like the rudders or hatch covers to achieve the sense of accomplishment that comes with a finished project.*

Now you need to plan out how the lines of the boat will look, these need to be pencilled out onto ply in full size. *This will start to give you an idea of the enormity of the project, and also show you just how much dry space you will need. By far the best result would be to have a barn that could be heated. I had to make do with sheets of polythene and extension cables. The winter was so cold and wet I had to halt construction. I got to know the radio like an old friend, and can still recall all the main hits of 1986-87.*

Draw out the shape of all the bulkheads and cut them out. *This is where I found out that learning carpentry at school would have been a good idea. You need good quality power tools. Only 25 years later did I find out what a router was! Also that hand saws need to be replaced every few hours of use. And cutting straight edges is not always the best thing for a curved hull. Edges need to be bevelled and all that fancy joinery stuff. A great investment is a top quality rechargeable drill/screwdriver and a jigsaw.*

Have a cup of tea. *Frequent breaks allow you to review efforts. Mistakes occur when you are tired out at the end of the day. A miss-cut section of ply will cost you time and money. Always measure twice and cut once. Offer up wherever possible. And be careful, once a hull toppled over on top of me because the props slipped. I was only saved by a luckily placed pile of tires. An infected cut will slow progress far more than cutting a little slower. Jigsaws particularly need sharp new blades and to find their own cutting pace. Wear safety glasses where appropriate. A builder or two have died when sleeping on board a poorly ventilated hull heated by a device producing carbon monoxide. Do not breathe in dust of any sort, wood or glue. Wear a top quality mask and change the filter often. Many Wharram builders succumb to epoxy allergies. You have to wear thick marigold gloves (thin latex is no good.)*

Create the stem and stern posts. *These stick up at the ends of the catamaran and give it its distinctive Polynesian feel. I stuck some fibreglass over the top of mine which was a mistake. Water always gets in and one post rotted after about five years and had to be replaced. When epoxy sheathing something it has to be dry, the air needs to be warm enough and not too humid. And the idea is to completely encapsulate the wood. Any gaps and the epoxy simply becomes a container from which the water cannot escape. Epoxy is not very UV proof so its needs treating. Sometimes it is better to use something like Burgess Wood seal so that the wood is always visible and any problems can be picked up before rot sets in.*

Cut out the ply backbone, the spine of the hulls running the whole length. *These laminated backbone strips give the boat its banana curve. A Wharram is based on a section of a great circle. Its general lines* match closely those of boats still found in the Pacific Islands. I treated these bits especially carefully with Cuprinol since water can gather in the hulls. A Wharram is supposed to be completely water-tight, bilge water needs to be got rid of. I avoided putting any holes through the hull for a toilet or instruments since these glands are always a source of trouble.

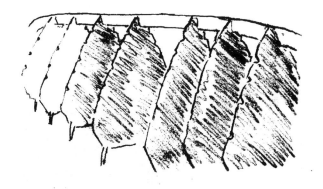

Now you have to join the bulkheads onto the backbone and make sure everything is square. *You might think that set squares and spirit levels would suffice, but because of the whip and bendiness of a half built frame you tend to rely on the eye. Eyeing everything up is vital. It's actually quite satisfying to work with your innate sense of balance and level. In fact the beauty of any boat depends on this kind of feel.*

How you need to mark out where all the stringers position on the bulkheads, and then glue, screw and nail them into place. *We used thousands of bronze gripfast nails on Jumble, but stainless screws were required where extra strength was needed. Never use inferior stainless, it weeps rust in the marine environment. Both copper and brass break quite quickly. The glue has to be waterproof, and is usually 'two part'. The stringers are made of soft wood. Later Wharram designs moved away from hardwood which is obviously endangered. Jumble though, was made of the highest quality hardwood marine ply. Only good marine ply does not delaminate in the wet. Exterior ply is not good enough if you want the best job.*

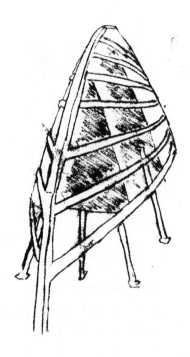

Now heave out all those sheets of ply and plank the hulls. Nails should be staggered on the stringers about two or three inches apart. You need someone dollying up on the inside to stop the ply springing away. *This is where having a decent sized shed comes into its own. I had to lug full size sheets of marine ply about 100ft from a garage to the boat. An 8ft by 4ft sheet was about at the limit of my stubby arms. This is an example of a job you simply cannot do on your own since you need to be both on the inside and the outside of the hull at the same time.*

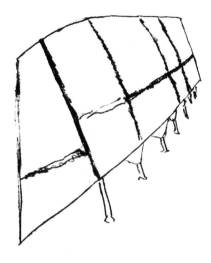

Plane all the edges of the ply level. *An electric plane or router helps here. By hand it is possible with a very sharp hand plane. Most of this works requires a keen eye. If the whole boat is on a level surface to begin with, it helps. Jumble was on a muddy slope (originally grass). By this time a builder has put in literally hundreds of hours, and may begin to ask "would it have been better to have taken on a renovation project or buy already built?" But now you are in too deeply to retreat, stamina is required. And another cup of tea!*

Outer keel ply is nailed and glued on and the laminated skeg put in place. *This is to beef up the hull where it needs it most. There is a tendency amongst homebuilders to over-engineer the craft. Stringers are made from slightly wider wood. Longer nails are used and more of them. Eventually the whole boat weighs twice as much as intended, sits low in the water and sails like a dog. So be careful before beefing up areas.*

Plane the keel to a rounded shape. *This is the part that has to slide up the sand, or bounce off that coral reef. On Jumble we originally screwed on a hardwood wear strip but this disintegrated after about 5 years and so we replaced it with stainless steel. This was sikaflexed and glued in place.*

The skeg is faired in. *The skeg fares in against the rudder which protrudes no lower. It is important that no rope can slip up between the skeg and the rudder. The smallest gap makes you vulnerable. We screwed on a stainless steel flange; this actually wore out quite quickly since it is the first thing in contact with, say, a concrete slipway. We did also try fairing the gap between the hull and the rudders with mylar flaps, on one boat the entire gap was filled with sikaflex. This lasted about a year.*

Sheath the hull the nylon fabric glued on without air pockets. One complete side needs to be completed per glue session. *This nightmare job requires complete dry, and warmth. We glued on 8 ounce nylon cloth with resorcinol glue, the problem is trying to remove all the air pockets. If these are missed then the bubbles have to be cut out, sanded till faired in, and resurfaced. The result is a coating that is impervious to wood boring worms. That fabric itself would probably hold together in the event of a collision, although we haven't yet put this to the test!*

Invite many friends over to roll the hulls upright. *Luckily there is something infectious about a boat being built on a shoestring, people like to get involved. It's a bit like holding a baby, ok whilst it smiles, but nice to hand back when it cries. At Tunbridge Wells we were blessed with the amazing generosity of the Bembridge's. They allowed large groups of boat builders to stay the night.*

Fix all the inner furniture. This stiffens the hull. *The furniture means things like bunks and shelving. A Tanenui is a very Spartan boat, the bunks are a little like coffins and there is only just headroom in about the middle two feet. On one side is the navigation area, and on the other the galley. We painted the roofs of the bunks white to create an impression of a little more space.*

Treat the hull with anti-rot paint. *We used a 1986 version of Cuprinol which contained all sorts of now prohibited substances. I later poured gallons of the stuff into the beam boxes which seemed like rot traps otherwise. Avoid all naked flames since the vapours are highly explosive. In fact be very careful with fire full stop. Epoxy burns furiously, several projects have succumbed to fire.*

Cut and fit the deck stringers into notches in the bulkheads. *Some of these stringers need to be planed to accommodate the bunk boards, or shelves that attach on them. Less than perfect joints I filled with a mixture of wood dust and glue. This technique was the act of last resort for the amateur carpenter. I had many last resorts.*
Add strengthening where the beams are going to sit. *I used wood larger than on the plan and this had all sort of knock on effects.*

Screw and glue on the decks. *The decks I covered in old nylon curtains stuck on with resorcinol glue. Only in 2006 did these start to delaminate. They ultimately need a coat of non-slip paint. We put sand in paint as a cheap alternative.*

Build the cabin tops and hatches. *A brief four words, but a lot of work. You actually build the cabin tops around a frame of softwood and have to saw a hole in it to gain access inside.*

Put in the windows. *Following advice we made the windows out of thick Perspex, and quite small. These were sikaflexed home and held in with a bolt every inch. They have never leaked. To cut Perspex is an art. Tape the lines to prevent shattering and use a very sharp, fast jigsaw. Experiment first since Perspex is expensive.*

Line up the two hulls. This involves making sure they are equally apart at both the stern and bow. Then use a line diagonally across to make sure things are not askew. *This can take ages, but it is vital to get it right. Out of line hulls will destroy a boats performance. By this stage of construction we were on the relatively level car park in Wimborne. Measure every which way. Once the decision is made that will be it forever!*

The prefabricated beam troughs can now be put in place. Then bolt them into place. *These beam troughs will have been prefabricated indoors during the winter months. Some Wharrams use flexible methods for holding the beams in place. Our Tanenui was designed to be rigid. We preferred this as a stiffer hull sails better.*

Laminate up the crossbeams from as good a timber as possible. *Complicated multilayer beams were abandoned as too expensive. In the end 13ft lengths of 4inch by 2inch timber were simply glued together. We used rough sawn timber reasoning that the glue would make a better bond.*

Now put the beams into the troughs and bolt them into place. *Once the beams were slotted in place they were out of reach. Partly because we had to hammer them in with sledge hammers. I cut a hole in the ends of all the beam troughs in the hope that this would prevent water from pooling and cause rot. For many years we plugged this hole at the end of the season and filled the troughs with Cuprinol.*

Screw on the bulwarks in a pleasing curve. Add a hardwood rubbing strip. *This job was estimated to take couple of days, in the end it took a couple of weeks. Part of the problem was curving the ply strips that made the bulwark and then finding a way of clamping them in place. Bill's brother succeeded in this and I never witnessed his secret method. The hardwood rubbing strip was in fact only semi-hardwood and did actually rot in places over the years.*

Mount the beams forward and aft for the netting. *We used a beautiful old gymnastics bar that I found in a Brighton skip. This was put on the bow. You can use sections of old aluminium masts.*

Build the decking in separate sections and screw into place. *Hardwood make these expensive and very heavy, we compromised by using softwood and two-part epoxy varnish which looked great for a number of years. Screwing them down is not ideal, it's better to also lash them so that a wave can't smash them off.*

Fabricate a tabernacle for the mast base to sit on. *Amazingly I bought the correct sized tabernacle at a local boat jumble quite early on. The best sort is a bespoke stainless steel one made out of tubing.*

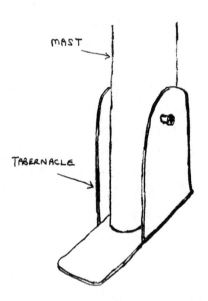

Bolt into place all the stainless chain plates. *This involves obtaining access to the back of bolts, since the lockers are quite small you need to be a bit of a contortionist. We drilled out the centres of coins as this was cheaper than buying washers. All our steel was hot galvanised and then coated with bitumenous epoxy.*

Laminate up the rudders. *This is a job for those long winter months. You have to be very careful that no twist develops.*

Attach the pintles for the rudders, and hang them. *We could find no factory made pintles that were anything like strong enough so we made them ourselves. The lower pins lasted about 15 years before wearing through.*

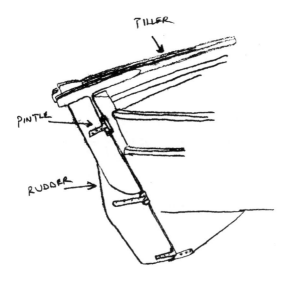

Build two tillers, incorporating Ackerman curves. *Another of those jobs which sound easy enough but are, in fact, very time consuming and difficult. One of the main problems being the laminated curve exploding apart before the glue could cure. This happened twice despite every vice and clamp in our possession being used.*

Construct a wooden mast from Sitka Spruce. *See the chapter devoted to this Herculean task. Frankly it would be easier to source a used aluminium one.*

Make stays from galvanised wire. *Galvanised wire has some advantages over stainless. It is cheaper and you can see where problems occur.*

Raise the mast, and employ rope lanyards *Obviously three helpers make this a lot safer. Rope gives the whole rig a little bit of flex.*

Have a set of sails made. *A skilled job well worth delegating. Shop around for the best quote.*

Build a pod for the outboard motor. *A job for the garden shed in the winter. Make it strong enough to resist the twisting moment of an engine in sudden reverse!*

Fit navigation lights. *When putting a wire up a mast try and stop it rattling. This is best done before the mast is raised. Smear frequent blobs of sikaflex along the wire as you thread it through, and allow it to rest on the horizontal mast until the mastic sets.*

Sew up splash proof foam cushions for the beds. *Use foam that does not compress too much.*

Construct a boom, reefing system and roller reefing for the foresail. *Our original boom was wood; this broke and was replaced with aluminium.*

Bolt on winches. *Two speed winches, as large as possible, are vital if you are going to cope with a genoa in any decent breeze.*

This just the broadest outline for what is involved in building a Wharram Tanenui.